Rip-Roaring Reads
for
Reluctant Teen Readers

Rip-Roaring Reads
for
Reluctant Teen Readers

Gale W. Sherman

Bette D. Ammon

1993
Libraries Unlimited, Inc.
Englewood, Colorado

Dedication

With thanks and love to terrific readers and wonderful daughters:
Ashley Sherman and Katie DeBruyne.

LIBRARIES UNLIMITED, INC.
P.O. Box 6633
Englewood, CO 80155-6633
1-800-237-6124

Library of Congress Cataloging-in-Publication Data

Sherman, Gale W.
    Rip-roaring reads for reluctant teen readers / Gale W. Sherman,
Bette D. Ammon.
    ix, 156 p. 22x28 cm.
    Includes bibliographical references and index.
    ISBN 1-56308-094-X
    1. Teenagers--United States--Books and reading. 2. Young adult
literature, English--Bibliography. I. Ammon, Bette DeBruyne.
II. Title.
Z1037.S524   1993
[PR990]
028.5'35--dc20   93-6439
                                                          CIP

Contents

Introduction

What makes anyone pick up a book to read? People who love to read have no problem answering that question; these readers voraciously devour all sorts of printed material and rarely travel anywhere without a book in hand. But a reluctant reader—someone who can read but chooses not to—poses a particular challenge to educators. A book has to be really special to capture that person's attention.

Most librarians, teachers, and parents strive to nurture lifelong literacy. We especially love encouraging students to willingly accept books as sources for real and lasting pleasure as well as sources for information. However, motivating those reluctant readers who have established patterns of nonreading is more difficult, yet critically important. Interrupting a nonreading cycle as early as possible is the charge. But what can we as parents and educators do to make reading as satisfying to a reluctant reader as it is to a book lover? How can we introduce nonreaders to exciting books that are impossible to put down?

Rip-Roaring Reads for Reluctant Teen Readers can answer these questions. The purpose of this book is to bring together books and readers and keep the reading process ongoing. By selecting forty contemporary, spellbinding books written by forty outstanding authors, we hope to make that matching process easier and more successful. Included are twenty rip-roaring reads for junior high school students or middle schoolers and twenty rip-roaring reads for high school students (grades nine through twelve). Interest and reading levels vary within each list, and many teachers, parents, and librarians will find books from both lists appropriate for individual students or class.

Selecting these forty titles was a particularly difficult task, and because no one list pleases everybody all of the time, it is inevitable that a "favorite" title has been omitted. Currently the abundance of reading material for children is remarkable and overwhelming, and recommended lists are ever-changing. In order to be included in *Rip-Roaring Reads*, the books had to have the following characteristics:

1. Recent publication date. Just like adult readers, young readers are attracted to new materials. Older "mustn't miss" titles for teen readers are included as further reading suggestions (see Bookmark explanations on page ix).

2. Relatively short length, preferably under 200 pages because thick books are sometimes daunting. However, we did not make "thinness" an overriding criterion. A highly motivated reader may be able to jump ahead at least two years in reading level.

3. Appealing format. Typeface and print size are attractive, with consideration given to page layout, paragraph length, amount of dialogue, and an attention-grabbing beginning. We avoided the look of traditional high-low books—a stigmatizing format with too-large print, poor-quality illustrations, overly wide margins, and so forth. Many of the books selected are available in paperback, which many teens prefer.

4. Eye-catching book jacket or cover with characters' ages accurately reflected.

5. High-interest, meaningful subject matter. Issues covered are topical, relevant, and captivating.

6. Appropriate reading level. Most of the books selected were calculated at reading levels between fourth and seventh grade. Again, realize that high interest will frequently attract and motivate a reader even though the text may be somewhat difficult.

7. Notable authors. Many of the authors selected are current teen favorites and are regularly included on recommended lists.

8. Excellent writing, vivid and realistic characters, authentic dialogue, and gripping plots.

Using This Book

The layout of the forty book entries enables the reader to scan the information quickly, view the books from various perspectives, and consider using the books in a variety of ways. The bibliographic data at the beginning of each entry not only is useful for ordering but contains other valuable information as well. For instance, the number of pages for each title is included. Adults looking for potential books for reluctant readers must pay particular attention to the length of books. Students who do not enjoy reading are concerned about the number of pages, regardless of how well a book is written.

Genres and Themes. Teens who elect not to read have preferences concerning the kinds of materials they would consider reading, just as they have preferences about their favorite television shows and music! Therefore, the genre selections for both age divisions are balanced and varied to help match students with books. Popular genres such as contemporary realistic fiction, mystery, and adventure are included, but so are biographies, informational books, and graphic novels. Every reader, reluctant or not, can find something rip-roaring to read.

Books fit into specific genres because of certain literary characteristics, whereas themes unify the plot, setting, and characters. More often than not, most stories can be categorized into two or more genres and have multiple underlying themes. Multiple genre and theme notations encourage looking at each book from as wide a perspective as possible. This increases the opportunities for its use in the classroom as well as for matching it with potential readers. Themes have been listed in order of importance.

Readability and Interest Levels. Because readability evaluations are subjective, results often vary. Using the Fry Readability Scale, reading levels were calculated for each book. The results give approximate reading levels, which need to be viewed in conjunction with the book's content, language style, and interest value.

Interest and readability levels frequently do not match. These rip-roaring reads were selected because they combined low readability levels and high interest levels. However, titles should not necessarily be dismissed if the reading level appears too high for your student or class. These may be perfect books to read aloud.

On the other hand, choices should not be limited. Even poor readers will attempt to read material above their reading levels if they are intensely interested in the subject. There is also a fine line between books that are easy and those that are too easy and, therefore, insulting. The more challenging book may be *the* book that changes a student from a reluctant reader to a devoted reader.

Reviews. Citations are listed for reviews appearing in the major journals that evaluate children's literature. These professional periodicals, which are the ones most readily accessible to librarians and teachers, are *Booklist*, *Bulletin of the Center for Children's Books*, *Horn Book*, *School Library Journal*, and *Voice of Youth Advocates* (*VOYA*).

The viewpoints expressed by the reviewers provide a range of opinions about the same work. If a book was starred or recommended in these journal reviews, that information has been included. These ratings are self-explanatory except for those of *VOYA*. The books *VOYA* reviews are rated for quality and popularity. They range from #1 ("Hard to understand how it got published" and "No young adult will read unless forced to for assignments") to #5 ("Hard to imagine it being better written" and "Every young adult [who reads] was dying to read it yesterday").

Author Information. Many students are intrigued by details about authors' lives. For instance, a reluctant reader who loves science fiction comic books may be persuaded to read a Ray Bradbury book simply because Bradbury was a Buck Rogers fan as a child. Or a reader fascinated with magic tricks may find Sid Fleischman's works appealing because he is a self-taught magician.

Plot Summary. Plot details are kept to a minimum. However, because most students prefer books with protagonists their own age or slightly older, the ages of the main characters are always stated or implied. Additional plot, setting, and character information can be gleaned from the themes, reviews, booktalks, and literature extension/alternative book report notations.

Introducing the Book. The hints in this section are intended to aid adults in sharing these books with individuals or groups of students. Many of these books would be good read-aloud candidates, and they are all good selections for independent reading by reluctant readers. We often recommend reading aloud a particular passage or specific chapter and note that in this section. These selections, ranging from a few paragraphs to twelve or fifteen pages, will grab potential readers.

Some books are not appropriate to read aloud because of sensitive and personal subject matter, while others are especially appropriate to share at certain times of the year. This information is included in this section. If a book appeared on the annual Recommended Books for the Reluctant Young Adult Reader list, that information is included. These titles are annually selected by the Reluctant Young Adult Reader Committee, Young Adult Library Services Association (YALSA) of the American Library Association (ALA).

Booktalks. Booktalking is a terrific way to sell books to potential readers. These talks should catch the listener's attention like "coming attractions" at the movies. They are "short and sweet" and not the same as book reviews, reports, or analyses. The "In the Aisle" booktalks are spontaneous sells suitable for grabbing a book off the shelf or doing many quick booktalks together. Tantalizing information is given, but few specific details are included.

Using excerpts from the text is the best way to give the true flavor of a book in a more prepared or traditional booktalk. "With the Author's Words" are booktalks that include a high-interest, quoted section from the book. When students see you read a selection from a book, they receive the nonverbal message that reading is pleasurable and that the pleasure comes from the book. Expect to sell these books when you booktalk! Don't disappoint students by not having the books available when you are finished. The canned, brief booktalks in *Rip-Roaring Reads* may be used in presentations or duplicated and used in book displays or on bulletin boards.

Literature Extensions/Alternative Book Report Activities. The recent trend toward whole language and literature-based curricula makes using "real" books an integral and welcome part of classroom activities. But please, forget the dreaded, boring book report as an accountability method. Instead, encourage students to look at alternative activities such as the ones listed in this book. However, don't think of these ideas as the only ones! Use these as a springboard to help you, your colleagues, *and* your students formulate other activities.

Don't be discouraged if your library doesn't have all the books recommended for further research or reading or both. In this day of limited budgets, no library will have them all, and that is why numerous choices are listed. To expand your materials collection, utilize interlibrary loan services, which most public libraries offer. Be sure, whatever you do, to *never* have a student spend more time on the extensions or activities than they did reading the book in the first place!

Bookmarks. Because the basic purpose of this book is to create lifelong readers, we want students to ask for more when they finish a title. After all, readers reading is the ultimate goal. These reproducible bookmarks will help you to match books with readers at a variety of reading levels and, most important, to hook them on books.

Each list includes books that extend reading experiences by listing other books by that author or other outstanding titles in a particular genre, theme, series, or topic area. The bookmarks include appropriate books for all readers, at a variety of reading levels.

Adapt these to your own individual needs, add titles from your library, or mark the titles you have in your collection or the titles available from another library in your area. Bookmarks need not be used only in connection with each specific entry. Each *Rip-Roaring Reads* entry has been listed on its appropriate bookmark, so use them anytime for all kinds of readers!

Appendix. The appendix lists all forty titles by interest level and readability level. Note the overlapping. Many books will appeal to students from middle school through high school.

Index. There are five indexes in this book. These include Genre, Curricular, Theme, Author, and Title. These indexes help librarians, teachers, and other adults make connections with books and assist them in matching readers with appropriate materials.

Good luck with your endeavors. Just one person can make a difference in a reluctant reader's life. Maybe that person is you. When book and reader meet, anything is possible. So introduce a few!

Rip-Roaring Reads
for
Junior High School Students

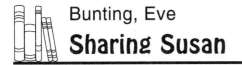

Bunting, Eve
Sharing Susan

LC 90-27097, ©1991, 122p., $12.95 (ISBN 0-0-06-021693-X; ISBN 0-06-2021694-8, library binding), HarperCollins

Genre: Contemporary realistic fiction

Themes: Parent-child relationships, babies switched at birth, death, fear, blood testing, compromise, negotiation, legal system

Reading level: Fourth grade

Interest level: Fifth through eighth grades

Reviews:
Booklist. 88(2):148 September 15, 1991
Horn Book. 68(1):68 January/February, 1992
School Library Journal. 37(10):120 October, 1991
Voice of Youth Advocates. 14(5):306 December, 1991. (#4 quality, #4 popularity)

Author Information

Eve Bunting was raised in Northern Ireland and cultivated her storytelling skills at a boarding school in Belfast (telling stories after lights out). Following her marriage, she lived in Scotland and then moved back to Ireland. In 1950, Bunting and her husband made the painful decision to immigrate to the United States. She and her husband and their daughter and two sons settled in Pasadena, California. Bunting received the Golden Kite Award from the Society of Children's Book Writers in 1976 for *One More Flight*. She writes nearly all the time, with many of her ideas for books coming from newspaper or magazine articles. Bunting says that for her "Writing is like breathing. It's just plain necessary." Bunting misses her Irish home and likes to write stories about Ireland.

Plot Summary

"The Big Worry" of why Susan's parents are acting so secretively is revealed when they tell her she may have been switched at birth with another baby. Susan's reaction is very emotional; she refuses to believe this could be true and can't conceive that her "parents" would even be willing to consider such a possibility. But a blood test confirms the accidental switch. The inevitable changes that result from this knowledge and the actions of both sets of parents, who wish to avoid a court battle, throw Susan into turmoil. Her ultimate acceptance of her new situation is precipitated by a frightening rescue.

Introducing the Book

Sharing Susan centers on a fascinating topic to both children and young adults. At one time or another many children wonder if they really belong in their families. Hook readers by reading aloud the first two chapters or using the booktalks below.

Booktalks

In the Aisle

Have you ever wondered if you're living with the right family? Susan never had until she finds out she might be living with the wrong family. But she's sure she doesn't want to be shared between two sets of parents. How could all this happen? Easily—two babies were accidentally switched at birth.

With the Author's Words

Susan has just learned that she might have been switched at birth with another baby, and she may be living with the wrong parents. She's determined not to switch families and confides in her best friend, Clemmie, who gives her some advice.

> *[Clemmie] had said something important yesterday, something I hadn't picked up on at the time, and I'd been going over and over it since. "Maybe they won't like you and they'll send you back," she'd said. Well, maybe I could make them not like me. How about that? It would sure be better than letting them all push me around.*
> (P. 42, hardback edition)

It sounds like *Sharing Susan* may not work out at all. Eve Bunting's book will keep you guessing.

Literature Extensions/Alternative Book Report Activities

Biology/Genetics—Susan and her parents must take blood tests to determine if they are her biological parents. By testing their blood, doctors can perform a chromosome test to determine parentage. To look further at this topic, invite a genetic engineer from a medical center or university to speak with your class. Students may be interested in gaining further knowledge about genetics, DNA, and blood testing.

Provide books such as Sandy Bornstein's *What Makes You What You Are: A First Look at Genetics* (Messner, 1989), *DNA Fingerprinting* by Christopher Lampton (Franklin Watts, 1991), Alvin Silverstein and Virginia B. Silverstein's *Genes, Medicine, and You* (Enslow, 1989), *The Virus Invaders* by Alan Nourse (Franklin Watts, 1992), and Frank H. Wilcox's *DNA: The Thread of Life* (Lerner, 1988).

Creative Writing—Eve Bunting often bases her books on articles she reads in magazines and newspapers. The story of a Florida child who was switched at birth may have been the impetus for *Sharing Susan*. Provide current newspapers and periodicals for students to peruse for articles of interest. Like Bunting, students can use a real event to create an expanded fictional story.

Creative Writing/Journals—Readers of *Sharing Susan* soon learn what "The Big Worry" is. Do your students have a "big worry" or lots of little ones? Allow students time to write privately on this topic in their journals. For journal writing ideas and assistance, consult *Journal Keeping with Young People* by Barbara Steiner and Kathleen C. Phillips (Libraries Unlimited, 1991).

Current Events—Using newspaper and periodical guides, students can research real incidents of infants being switched at birth. Compare and contrast these events to the fictional account depicted in *Sharing Susan*.

Eve Bunting Wrote:

Coffin on a Case

The Face at the Edge of the World

The Ghost Children

The Haunting of Safekeep

The Hide-Out

If I Asked You, Would You Stay?

In the Haunted House

Jumping the Nail

Our Sixth-Grade Sugar Babies

Sharing Susan

Such Nice Kids

A Sudden Silence

Will You Be My POSSLQ?

Dear Susan Books with Letters

Bunting, Eve. *Sharing Susan*

Byars, Betsy. *Bingo Brown, Gypsy Lover*

Cleary, Beverly. *Dear Mr. Henshaw*

Conford, Ellen. *Dear Lovey Hart: I Am Desperate!*

Kline, Suzy. *Orp and the Chop Suey Burgers*

Leedy, Loreen. *Messages in the Mailbox: How to Write a Letter*

MacLachlan, Patricia. *Sarah, Plain and Tall*

Marriott, Janice. *Letters to Lesley*

Who Are Your Parents?

Bunting, Eve. *Sharing Susan*

Cooney, Caroline B. *The Face on the Milk Carton*

Corcoran, Barbara. *Family Secrets*

Covington, Vicki. *Gathering Home*

Holland, Isabelle. *The House in the Woods*

MacDonald, Caroline. *Speaking to Miranda*

Martin, Ann M. *Missing Since Monday*

Mazer, Norma Fox. *The Taking of Terri Mueller*

Okimoto, Jean Davies. *Molly by Any Other Name*

Pfeffer, Susan Beth. *Most Precious Blood*

Byars, Betsy
Bingo Brown, Gypsy Lover

LC 89-48714, ©1990, 122p., $11.95 (ISBN 0-670-83322-3), Viking. Paperback $3.99 (ISBN 0-14-03451803), Puffin Books

Genres: Contemporary realistic fiction, humor

Themes: Boy-girl relationships, family life, peer relationships, pregnancy, newborns, grandparents, letter writing

Reading level: Fourth grade

Interest level: Fifth through eighth grades

Reviews:
Booklist. 86(17):1699 May 1, 1990. (Starred)
Bulletin of the Center for Children's Books. 43(10):234 June, 1990. (Recommended)
Horn Book. 66(4):453 July/August, 1990
School Library Journal. 36(6):117 June, 1990. (Starred)

Author Information

Born in 1928 in North Carolina, Betsy Byars currently lives in South Carolina. Throughout her writing career, Byars has penned (or word processed) over thirty books, averaging a book per year. She has won numerous awards and continues to be a popular author for middle school readers. Her personal interests include aviation (she earned a pilot's license in 1984), volunteering in public libraries, and tutoring children with learning difficulties. Well-known for her funny stories, Byars tried once to write a purely humorous book but discovered she needed a serious theme as a base before she added the humor. She never intended the Bingo Brown series to be funny but says that it just happened. Byars says she has fun writing the Bingo Brown books because "I don't have to sit there for hours thinking, now what can he do, because he just does stuff on his own." A memoir of Byars's childhood is available in her book *The Moon and I* (Messner, 1991).

Plot Summary

Sixth-grader Bingo Brown has another star-studded performance in the third book of the Bingo Brown series. Coping with his long-distance romance and worrying about what Christmas present would be appropriate for his faraway sweetheart are just two of his problems. Bingo is convinced his arms are proportionally growing out of control; he's concerned about his mother's difficult pregnancy; and he must deal with the unwanted affections of Boots, a girl in his school. With his usual aplomb, Bingo sorts through all these difficulties in this laugh-out-loud novel.

Introducing the Book

The entire book is a terrific read-aloud. To hook potential readers, however, simply read all of chapter 1 aloud. Boys *and* girls will enjoy the humor and identify with Bingo's multiple worries. Because the action takes place prior to Christmas vacation, consider introducing the book then. Remind fans that there are three other Bingo Brown books in the series.

Booktalks

In the Aisle

This third book about Bingo Brown may be the funniest yet. He's worrying about his faraway girlfriend, his pregnant mother, and the way his body seems to be growing—his arms are out of control! What is a "gypsy lover" anyway?

With the Author's Words

Bingo is sure his arms are growing out of control and is trying to convince his mother of the seriousness of his problem. His mother tells him he is supposed to be growing.

> *"I'm supposed to grow, but all together! Not in parts! A person's not supposed to grow two long arms and then two adult ears and then size-twelve feet!"*
> *"Bingo-"*
> *"Growing's supposed to be a natural thing that you don't even notice. And what if it keeps on—did you ever stop to think of that? What if my arms keep getting longer and longer, because that's exactly what they feel like they're doing! Then what?"*
> (Pp. 15-16, hardback edition)

His arms aren't the only thing out of control in Bingo's life. And how on earth can Bingo Brown be a gypsy lover? Betsy Byars's rollicking story will tickle your funny bone.

Literature Extensions/Alternative Book Report Activities

Health/Human Growth and Development—Bingo is concerned about his adolescent growth pattern, manifested in rapidly growing arms. He also is interested in the development of his family's new baby.

Provide books that answer questions about the human body and its growth patterns. Some are *What's Happening to My Body? Book for Boys: A Growing Up Guide for Parents and Sons* by Lynda Madaras and Dane Saavedra (Newmarket, 1987), *Everything You Need to Know About Growing Up Male* by Bruce Glassman (Rosen, 1991), *Your Growing Child* (Time Life, 1987), and *A Child Is Born* by Lennart Nilsson (Delacorte Press, 1990). Also available is the Emmy-award-winning video, *The Miracle of Life* (Ambrose Video, 1988), in which Swedish photographer Lennart Nilsson's camera goes inside human reproductive organs.

Home Economics/Cooking—Bingo Brown is an expert fudge maker. Provide students with Ian Fleming's *Chitty, Chitty Bang Bang* (Random House, 1964) and its excellent fudge recipe. Other interesting recipe books are Jill Krementz's *The Fun of Cooking* (Alfred A. Knopf, 1985), which features recipes by kids who love to cook; *Better Homes and Gardens Step-by-Step Kids' Cook Book* (Better Homes and Gardens, 1984); *Better Homes and Gardens After-School Cook Book* (Better Homes and Gardens, 1987); and *My First Baking Book: A Life-size Guide to Baking Delicious Things to Eat* by Helen Drew (Alfred A. Knopf, 1991).

Language Arts/Letter Writing—Bingo's correspondence with Melissa is a major event in both their lives. Provide a collection of other books in which letter writing is a major theme. These might include *The Letter, the Witch and the Ring* by John Bellairs (Dial Press, 1976), Beverly Cleary's *Dear Mr. Henshaw* (Morrow Junior Books, 1983), *The War Began at Supper: Letters to Miss Loria* by Patricia Reilly Giff (Delacorte Press, 1991), *Dear Readers and Riders* by Marguerite Henry (Rand McNally, 1969), F.N. Monjo's *Letters to Horseface: Young Mozart's Travels in Italy* (Viking, 1975), and "Letters from a Concentration Camp" by Yohkilo Uchida in *The Big Book for Peace* (Dutton Children's Books, 1990). Also, share Janet Ahlberg and Allan Ahlberg's unique books *The Jolly Postman* (Little, Brown, 1986) and *The Jolly Christmas Postman* (Little, Brown, 1991). Students can use them as models for creating their own unusual books featuring letters.

Consult "Reading the Mail—Books About Letters," *Book Links*, 1(3): 40-46, January, 1992, for further literature extensions.

Language Arts/Writing—Bingo is good at giving advice and apparently is a fan of the "Dear Abby" columns (P. 108, hardback edition). Provide samples of "Dear Abby" and other advice columns, such as those in popular teen magazines. As an activity have students anonymously submit letters depicting real or fictitious problems that will be answered by other individuals or groups of students. Share aloud or publish the results.

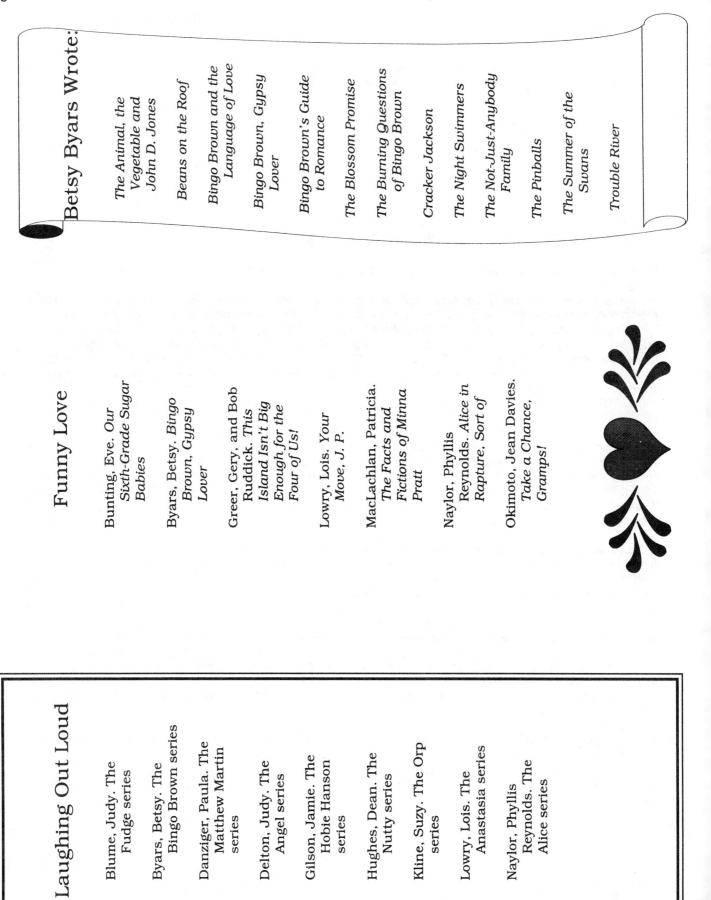

Betsy Byars Wrote:

The Animal, the Vegetable and John D. Jones

Beans on the Roof

Bingo Brown and the Language of Love

Bingo Brown, Gypsy Lover

Bingo Brown's Guide to Romance

The Blossom Promise

The Burning Questions of Bingo Brown

Cracker Jackson

The Night Swimmers

The Not-Just-Anybody Family

The Pinballs

The Summer of the Swans

Trouble River

Funny Love

Bunting, Eve. *Our Sixth-Grade Sugar Babies*

Byars, Betsy. *Bingo Brown, Gypsy Lover*

Greer, Gery, and Bob Ruddick. *This Island Isn't Big Enough for the Four of Us!*

Lowry, Lois. *Your Move, J. P.*

MacLachlan, Patricia. *The Facts and Fictions of Minna Pratt*

Naylor, Phyllis Reynolds. *Alice in Rapture, Sort of*

Okimoto, Jean Davies. *Take a Chance, Gramps!*

Laughing Out Loud

Blume, Judy. The Fudge series

Byars, Betsy. The Bingo Brown series

Danziger, Paula. The Matthew Martin series

Delton, Judy. The Angel series

Gilson, Jamie. The Hobie Hanson series

Hughes, Dean. The Nutty series

Kline, Suzy. The Orp series

Lowry, Lois. The Anastasia series

Naylor, Phyllis Reynolds. The Alice series

Cleary, Beverly
Strider

LC 90-00608, ©1991, 179p., $12.95 (ISBN 0-440-84585-8), Morrow Junior Books. Paperback $3.99 (ISBN 0-380-71236-9) Avon Books

Genre: Contemporary realistic fiction

Themes: Single-parent families, friendship, dogs, problem solving, responsibility, joint custody, diaries, abandonment, goals, high school, peer relationships, boy-girl relationships, self-acceptance

Reading level: Fourth grade

Interest level: Fifth through eighth grades

Reviews:
Booklist. 87(21):2041 July, 1991. (Starred)
Bulletin of the Center for Children's Books. 45(2):34 October, 1991. (Recommended)
Horn Book. 67(5):595-96 September/October, 1991
School Library Journal. 37(9):250 September, 1991

Author Information
Born in 1916, Beverly Cleary grew up in Oregon. She was in the low reading group (the Blackbirds not the Bluebirds or Redbirds) until third grade. One dull and rainy Sunday, Cleary was excited to discover the Sunday-school library and find fun books to read. This signaled her birth as a reader. Even then it was suggested that Cleary should be a writer of children's books when she grew up, and that became her ambition. Cleary wanted to write the kind of books she loved to read: funny stories about children like those she knew. After attending college, Cleary became a children's librarian—"the next best thing to a writer." *Henry Huggins* (Morrow Junior Books) was her first book, published in 1950. Since then, Cleary has continued to be a popular author, winning numerous awards. Her first story about Leigh Botts was the Newbery Award winner, *Dear Mr. Henshaw* (Morrow Junior Books, 1983). The idea for that book came from letters Cleary received from several boys who asked her "to write a book about a boy whose parents are divorced." For details about Cleary's childhood, consult her autobiography, *A Girl from Yamhill* (Morrow Junior Books, 1988).

Plot Summary
Strider begins when fourteen-year-old Leigh Botts rediscovers the diary he started in *Dear Mr. Henshaw* (Morrow Junior Books, 1983). Since the events of that book, he has mostly adjusted to life with his single-parent mom and only occasional visits from his father. Money continues to worry Leigh's mother, but she and Leigh have a strong relationship and successfully handle their life together. Leigh and his best friend, Barry, adopt a dog abandoned on the beach. Because Leigh and his mother have a strict landlady, joint custody seems to be the only way Leigh can share Strider's ownership. In spite of difficulties in sharing the dog, Leigh becomes a responsible pet owner. As he begins high school, Leigh's self-confidence improves with his participation on the track team, his increasing circle of friends, and his friend Strider running at his side.

Introducing the Book
This sequel to *Dear Mr. Henshaw* can be read in tandem with the first book or by itself. The occasional illustrations are at times awkward but provide relief for very reluctant readers. The chapters are short and the print is quite large. Because the action begins the summer before Leigh starts high school, this book is a winner for all middle schoolers. As an introduction, read aloud from page 1 to near the bottom of page 9 (hardback edition), ending with "and I haven't even come to the good part."

Booktalks

In the Aisle
Leigh worries. He worries about starting high school, making the track team, girls, and keeping his dog, Strider, a secret. When he and his best friend, Barry, agree to share ownership of Strider, everyone says it will never work. But for a while it did and now ... well, maybe everybody else was right.

With the Author's Words
The abandoned dog on the beach with no collar and no tags reminded Leigh of his old dog.

> "Hi, dog," [I] thought of my ex-dog Bandit and the fun we used to have before the divorce, when Mom got me and Dad got Bandit.... "Come on, fella." The dog didn't move. I scratched his chest where Bandit liked to be scratched. This dog looked up at me with his ears laid back and the saddest look I have ever seen on a dog's face. If dogs could cry, this dog would be crying hard. (Pp. 11-12, hardback edition)

This is the beginning of an important friendship between Leigh and this dog. They really need each other. But *Strider* is more than a dog story. It's the story of Leigh and his ninth-grade year and how the dog Strider actually helps Leigh succeed.

Literature Extensions/Alternative Book Report Activities

Art—In Barry's house, a kitchen wall is decorated with cooked spaghetti. Family members throw spaghetti against the wall to see if it is finished cooking. If it sticks to the wall, it's done. "When enough spaghetti has stuck to the wall, they spray-paint over it and start again" (p. 37, hardback edition). Students can create similar modern art projects on a variety of surfaces and paint them creatively. An alternative project would be to create mosaics with varieties of uncooked pasta.

Language Arts/Media Literacy—Leigh's mother has relaxed her anti-TV attitude because his grades are good and he is a discriminating viewer. Most people watch too much television and have few skills when it comes to critical television viewing or media literacy. Media literacy is the ability to effectively evaluate, analyze, and produce media in a variety of forms including television. Teach students to be active viewers, thinking critically about the information they receive from television programming and advertisements. When television is used constructively, it provides excellent opportunities for learning.

Useful periodicals for teachers include *Strategies*, a quarterly publication from Strategies for Media Literacy, Inc., Suite 410, 1095 Market Street, San Francisco, CA 94103, (415) 621-2911; *ADBUSTERS Quarterly*, 1243 West 7th Avenue, Vancouver, BC Canada V6H 1B7, (604) 736-9401; and *Media Matters*, a newsletter from the National Council for Teachers of English, c/o Robert Happ, Hempstead High School, 3715 Pennsylvania Avenue, Dubuque, IA 52001.

Refer also to *Taming the Wild Tube* by Robert L. Schrag (University of North Carolina Press, 1990), *Teleliteracy: Taking Television Seriously* by David Bianculli (Continuum Press, 1992), and Marie Winn's *The Plug-In Drug* (Viking, 1985) and *Unplugging the Plug-In Drug* (Viking, 1987).

Language Arts/Writing—Leigh Botts derives great satisfaction from daily writing in his diary and is challenged by the writing assignments he receives in school. Examples of his compositions can be found on pages 87-88, hardback edition ("The old man said ... I don't care aboucher dog") and pages 172-173, hardback edition ("Sunshines ... I rejoice").

Provide some of the current writing guides intended for use by students and teachers to help improve student writing skills. A few titles are *What's Your Story?: A Young Person's Guide to Writing Fiction* by Marion Dane Bauer (Clarion Books, 1992), *Real Toads in Imaginary Gardens: Suggestions and Starting Points for Young Creative Writers* by Stephen Phillip Policoff and Jeffrey Skinner (Chicago Review Press, 1991), *In Your Own Words: A Beginner's Guide to Writing* by Sylvia Cassedy (HarperCollins Children's Books, 1990), *Clear and Lively Writing: Creative Ideas and Activities, Grades 6-10* by Beth Means and Lindy Lindner (Libraries Unlimited, 1988), and *Kids Have All the Write Stuff: Inspiring Your Children to Put Pencil to Paper* by Sharon A. Edwards and Robert W. Maloy (Viking Penguin, 1992).

For specific information about journal writing, consult *Journal Keeping with Young People* by Barbara Steiner and Kathleen C. Phillips (Libraries Unlimited, 1991).

Social Studies/Animal Control—Every community has to deal with abandoned pets and uncontrolled animal populations. What happens to these animals in your area? What efforts are being made to educate pet owners about ownership responsibilities? Students can research and report on the financial costs of pet control and animal euthanasia in their communities. Compare and contrast these figures to national averages. What can be done to improve the situation in your area?

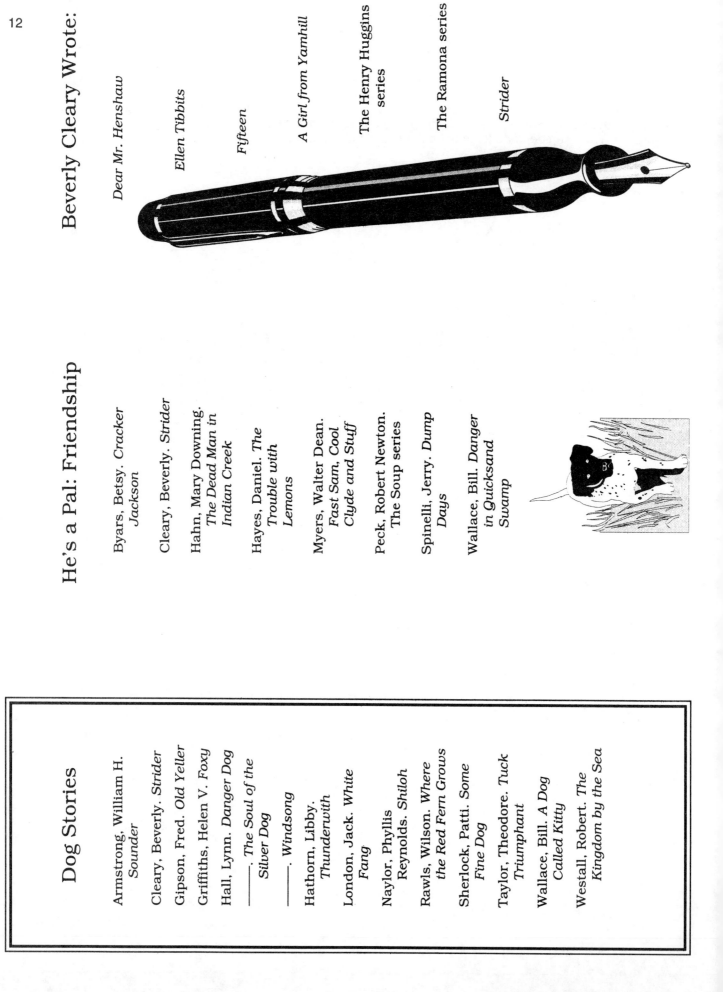

Beverly Cleary Wrote:

Dear Mr. Henshaw

Ellen Tibbits

Fifteen

A Girl from Yamhill

The Henry Huggins series

The Ramona series

Strider

He's a Pal: Friendship

Byars, Betsy. *Cracker Jackson*

Cleary, Beverly. *Strider*

Hahn, Mary Downing. *The Dead Man in Indian Creek*

Hayes, Daniel. *The Trouble with Lemons*

Myers, Walter Dean. *Fast Sam, Cool Clyde and Stuff*

Peck, Robert Newton. The Soup series

Spinelli, Jerry. *Dump Days*

Wallace, Bill. *Danger in Quicksand Swamp*

Dog Stories

Armstrong, William H. *Sounder*

Cleary, Beverly. *Strider*

Gipson, Fred. *Old Yeller*

Griffiths, Helen V. *Foxy*

Hall, Lynn. *Danger Dog*

———. *The Soul of the Silver Dog*

———. *Windsong*

Hathorn, Libby. *Thunderwith*

London, Jack. *White Fang*

Naylor, Phyllis Reynolds. *Shiloh*

Rawls, Wilson. *Where the Red Fern Grows*

Sherlock, Patti. *Some Fine Dog*

Taylor, Theodore. *Tuck Triumphant*

Wallace, Bill. *A Dog Called Kitty*

Westall, Robert. *The Kingdom by the Sea*

Conrad, Pam
Stonewords: A Ghost Story

LC 89-36382, ©1990, 130p., $13.95 (ISBN 0-06-021311-9; ISBN 0-06-021316-7, library binding), HarperCollins. Paperback $3.95 (ISBN 0-06-440377-7), Trophy

Genres: Mystery/supernatural, contemporary realistic fiction

Themes: Ghosts, time travel, friendship, love, grandparents, responsibility, courage, abandonment

Reading level: Fifth grade

Interest level: Fifth through ninth grades

Reviews:
Booklist. 86(13):1338 March 1, 1990
Bulletin of the Center for Children's Books. 43(9):211 May, 1990. (Recommended and starred)
Horn Book. 66(5):600 September/October, 1990
School Library Journal. 36(5):103 May, 1990. (Starred)
Voice of Youth Advocates. 13(2):101 June, 1990. (#3 quality, #3 popularity)

Author Information

Pam Conrad's writing began with a childhood bout of chicken pox. Her mother gave her paper, expecting her to draw, but she proceeded to write poetry instead. Conrad continued to write sporadically throughout junior and senior high school, writing what she describes as "mostly love poems and stories about girls who would perform acts of great sacrifice." Taking time off to get married and have children, Conrad didn't really start writing again until her children were in school and she had returned to college. Her books are not strictly autobiographical, but they do tell a little about her life. Conrad was born in New York in 1947 and now lives in Rockville Centre, New York, with her teenage daughter who draws. They hope to someday join talents on a picture book.

Plot Summary

Left with her grandparents at age four, Zoe makes friends with a ghost named Zoe Louise from 1870. Their friendship continues for years while Zoe grows and matures, but Zoe Louise remains a child, frozen in time on the day of her eleventh birthday and her imminent death. Zoe becomes determined to save her friend from her death before it happens. But, in order to do so, Zoe must travel through the time warp that exists in the mysterious back stairway.

Introducing the Book

This scary story won't take much selling and will please pre-Stephen King and Christopher Pike-R. L. Stine book lovers. To entice readers, read aloud from the first page to the break on page 15 (hardback edition) or to the end of chapter 2.

Booktalks

In the Aisle

Day is night and night is day as the two Zoes move between each other's worlds and time as visiting ghosts. But time is short, and the present-day Zoe will have to take action quickly if she is to save her friend of the past from a premature death.

With the Author's Words

Zoe recounts her first attempt to time travel through the stairway door to visit her ghost friend:

> I braced myself, stood ... took a deep breath, and with both hands leading, pressed through the door, my hands and my wrists all disappearing from me, my forearms, my elbows gone, and then I pressed my face to the door. Nothing resisted. Nothing stopped me. My face pushed through the door like the most natural thing in the world until I was halfway through up to my waist. I froze in terror. (Pp. 48-49, hardback edition)

It may take more courage than Zoe possesses to do this kind of traveling. Will she be caught between times? Will she make it through? And, if she does, will she be able to return to the present? Pam Conrad's *Stonewords: A Ghost Story* might keep you up at night!

Literature Extensions/Alternative Book Report Activities

Art—Zoe's mother names her after a name she read on an old tombstone. Visit a cemetery in your area, preferably an old one. Teach students how to do a tombstone rubbing using various types of paper and wax crayons. For further information refer to books such as *Creative Rubbings* by Laye Andrew (Watson-Guptill, 1968).

History—Zoe discovers a cache of old newspapers from the 1870s in her grandparents' cellar. The family spends hours reading and sharing articles of interest with each other. Most libraries have historic newspapers on microfilm, microfiche, or in hard copy. Depending on the newspaper holdings in your library, choose a variety of dates and write them on slips of paper. Students can randomly select a date to research and report on the happenings of that day.

Literature/Discussion—Following the reading of *Stonewords*, have students read Philippa Pearce's *Tom's Midnight Garden* (J.B. Lippincott, 1984) or *Wait Till Helen Comes: A Ghost Story* by Mary Downing Hahn (Clarion Books, 1986) or both. These three books have much in common. Comparing and contrasting them will stimulate an interesting literary discussion.

Research/Haunted Houses—Many students are fascinated by the possibility of the existence of ghosts and haunted houses. Have these students spend some time in school and public libraries discovering how to locate and select books and articles on this topic. Each student can share the results of his or her research in bibliographic form. As a further extension, some students can write annotated entries to combine in a collective bibliography to share with others. See the Bookmark Scary Stuff—Haunted Houses, included in the Joan Lowery Nixon *Whispers from the Dead* entry on page 123 for books about real haunted houses.

Pam Conrad Wrote:

Holding Me Here

My Daniel

Prairie Songs

Seven Silly Circles

Staying Nine

Stonewords: A Ghost Story

Taking the Ferry Home

The Tub People

What I Did for Roman

Absent Parents

Conrad, Pam. *Stonewords: A Ghost Story*

Corcoran, Barbara. *Stay Tuned*

Fitzhugh, Louise. *Sport*

Fox, Paula. *Monkey Island*

Grant, Cynthia D. *Keep Laughing*

Hermes, Patricia. *Mama, Let's Dance*

Hill, Kirkpatrick. *Toughboy and Sister*

MacLachlan, Patricia. *Journey*

Ghostly Time Travel

Conrad, Pam. *Stonewords: A Ghost Story*

Cresswell, Helen. *Moondial*

Levin, Betty. *Marcy's Mill*

Lunn, Janet. *The Root Cellar*

MacDonald, Reby Edmond. *The Ghosts of Austwick Manor*

Marzollo, Jean. *Halfway Down Paddy Lane*

Peck, Richard. The Blossom Culp series

Reiss, Kathryn. *Time Windows*

Voigt, Cynthia. *Building Blocks*

Wright, Betty Ren. *A Ghost in the House*

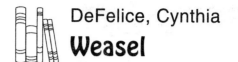

DeFelice, Cynthia
Weasel

LC 89-37794, ©1990, 112p., $11.95 (ISBN 0-02-726457-2), Macmillan. Paperback $3.50 (ISBN 0-380-71358-6), Avon Camelot

Genres: Historical fiction, adventure

Themes: Families, pioneer life (Ohio, 1839), good versus evil, revenge, Indian hunters, coming of age, cruelty, hatred, hunting, survival, wilderness

Readability: Fourth grade

Interest Level: Fifth through ninth grades. (Though the main character is eleven years old, the intense subject matter will appeal to older students.)

Reviews:
Booklist. 43(9):1799 May 15, 1990
Bulletin of the Center for Children's Books. 43(9):212 May, 1990
School Library Journal. 36(5):104 May, 1990. (Starred)
Voice of Youth Advocates. 13(1):101-02 June, 1990. (#3 quality, #3 popularity)

Author Information

Now a professional storyteller and a member of the Wild Washerman team, Cynthia DeFelice previously was a school librarian. She makes appearances at libraries, workshops, festivals, and schools. DeFelice was raised with books; her mother was an English teacher. The books DeFelice liked best as a child were the ones that made her feel as if she "was right in the story, part of what was happening," she says. With her own writing, she says she attempts to "create an illusion of reality," but she sees her primary task as providing entertainment. "So I want to entertain, I want to keep my readers turning those pages! But I also want to leave them with a memory worth having, with characters they will remember and ideas they will come back to." Living in Geneva, New York, DeFelice and her husband have two children.

Plot Summary

When eleven-year-old Nathan and his young sister, Molly, travel with the strange and silent Ezra to find their injured father, they learn the horrible truth about the cruel Indian hunter, Weasel. He's responsible for Ezra's tragedy and many other miseries inflicted on innocent people. Nathan is captured by Weasel but escapes and rejoins his family. The desire for revenge eats away at Nathan; he wishes he had killed Weasel when he had the chance. Nathan's hatred of Weasel dissolves with the gradual realization that Weasel's death would not erase the grief he caused.

Introducing the Book

In order to hook potential readers, read to the end of chapter 1 and stop, or continue on to any of a dozen other gripping places when attention has been captured. The tone of the book is stark and the language almost poetic. Some aspects of the novel are violent and gruesome, but the presentation of moral choices and unhappy truths of frontier settlement should provoke interesting and valuable discussions and debate. Complicated issues are put forth clearly and even the youngest reader or listener will grasp the ideas presented.

Booktalks

In the Aisle

You might think this book is about an animal—a weasel. Well, it isn't. It's about a man who's so sneaky he's nicknamed Weasel. He's also a cold-hearted killer. Nathan, the boy in this story, comes face-to-face with him.

With the Author's Words

> *The State of Ohio, 1839 ... The dogs were dozing in their usual places by the fire when the knock came. My sister, Molly, and I jumped. Who could be stopping at our cabin, so deep in the woods, so far from town, so late at night? (P. 1, hardback edition)*

Weasel by Cynthia DeFelice begins. The journeys and terrifying discoveries made by Nathan and his sister, Molly, will keep you riveted until the end.

Literature Extensions/Alternative Book Report Activities

Handicrafts—Although he is a white man, Ezra has adopted a Native American style of living as described on page 12. Students could use old methods to create something similar to Ezra's clothes and lifestyle. See page 12 with descriptions of Ezra's moccasins (beadwork and quills), necklaces, shirt, and leggings.

Refer to books such as *Indian Crafts and Skills: An Illustrated Guide for Making Authentic Indian Clothing, Shelters, and Ornaments* by David R. Montgomery (Horizon, 1985), *Native American Crafts Workshop* by Bonnie Bernstein and Leigh Blair (Fearon Teacher Aids, 1982), *The Book of Indian Crafts and Indian Lore* by Julian Harris Salomon (Harper & Brothers, 1928), *The Spark in the Stone: Skills and Projects from the Native American Tradition* by Peter Goodchild (Chicago Review Press, 1991), and *Indian Art in America: The Arts and Crafts of the North American Indian* by Frederick J. Duckstader (New York Graphic Society, 1961).

History—Both novels and informational books have been written about the attempted resettlement of American Indians as the white settlers moved steadily westward. In particular, the forced relocation of the Cherokee people is well chronicled and referred to as "the Trail of Tears."

For moving accounts of this incident, provide students with Dee Alexander Brown's novel *Creek Mary's Blood* (Holt, 1980) and the following nonfiction books: *The Cherokee Removal, 1838: An Entire Indian Nation Is Forced Out of Its Homeland* by Glenn Fleischmann (Franklin Watts, 1971), *Trail of Tears: The Rise and Fall of the Cherokee Nation* by John Ehle (Doubleday, 1988), *Trail of Tears: American Indians Driven from Their Lands* by Jeanne Williams (Hendrick-Long, 1992), and *The Story of the Trail of Tears* by R. Conrad Stein and David S. Catrow (Childrens Press, 1988).

Issues—As mentioned above in the "Introducing the Book" section, this short novel can provide grist for the discussion mill. Is DeFelice's book an argument against the death penalty? What about "frontier justice"? These issues—capital punishment, revenge, and so on—are always topical. Use this novel as a springboard for further research and discussion. Students can also compare and contrast the themes in *Weasel* with issues of justice versus civil disobedience depicted in K. M. Peyton's *Poor Badger* (Delacorte Press, 1992).

Language Arts/Tall Tales—Nathan and his friends often reenacted some of the incredible stories they had heard about Daniel Boone. Tales they heard and told about Weasel had achieved "tall tale" status in this book. Compare stories about Pecos Bill, Paul Bunyan, Johnny Appleseed, and Daniel Boone with the tales the children told about Weasel. How does the truth become stretched and why do these characters become larger than life? What is it we remember about stories told to us—the exaggerations?

I'm Going to Get You! Tales of Revenge

Manguel, Alberto, ed. *Dark Arrows: Chronicles of Revenge*

Muskopf, Elizabeth. *The Revenge of Jeremiah Plum*

O'Dell, Scott, and Elizabeth Hall. *Thunder Rolling in the Mountains*

Paige, Harry W. *Shadow on the Sun*

Taylor, Theodore. *Sniper*

Wallace, Bill. *Danger in Quicksand Swamp*

Indian Boys: Tales of the Past

Baird, Thomas. *Walk Out a Brother*

Blades, Anne. *A Boy of Tache*

Cazzola, Gus. *To Touch the Deer*

Chester, Diane. *The Sign of the Owl*

DeFord, Deborah H., and Harry S. Stout. *An Enemy Among Them*

Dickinson, Peter. *Annerton Pit*

Fleischman, Paul. *Saturnalia*

Hudson, Jan. *Dawn Rider*

Luhrmann, Winifred Bruce. *Only Brave Tomorrows*

Moore, Ruth Nulton. *Wilderness Journey*

Speare, Elizabeth. *The Sign of the Beaver*

If you loved *Weasel* by Cynthia DeFelice, you will like:

Avi. *Night Journeys*

Bauer, Marion Dane. *On My Honor*

Blackwood, Gary. *Wild Timothy*

Gregory, Kristiana. *The Legend of Jimmy Spoon*

Lawlor, Laurie. *Daniel Boone*

O'Dell, Scott. *Sing Down the Moon*

O'Dell, Scott, and Elizabeth Hall. *Thunder Rolling in the Mountains*

Rockwood, Joyce. *To Spoil the Sun*

Speare, Elizabeth. *The Sign of the Beaver*

Wisler, G. Clifton. *The Raid*

Fleischman, Sid
The Midnight Horse

LC 89-23441, ©1990, 84p., $12.95 (ISBN 0-0-688009441-4), Greenwillow Books

Genres: Adventure, fantasy

Themes: Magicians, orphans, ghosts, good versus evil, swindlers, rumors, inheritance, villains

Reading level: Fourth grade

Interest level: Third through seventh grades

Reviews:
Booklist. 86(22):2171 August, 1990. (Starred)
Bulletin of the Center for Children's Books.
    44(4):83 December, 1990. (Recommended)
Horn Book. 66(6):744 November/December,
    1990
School Library Journal. 36(9):226 September,
    1990. (Starred)

Author Information
A self-trained magician via books from the public library, Sid Fleischman became an expert at sleight-of-hand tricks and later brought this talent to his writing. New York-born in 1920, Fleischman grew up in San Diego and learned storytelling from his European father. Fleischman has maintained his interest in magic and has been writing since he was nineteen. Fleischman is father to Paul Fleischman, another popular, award-winning children's author, and two daughters. His children inherited his enchantment with words and loved following the adventures of his various characters as their father read aloud to them from works in progress.

Plot Summary
When orphan Touch arrives in Cricklewood, New Hampshire, to meet his only relative, Judge Wigglesforth, he finds a magician ghost, a damsel in distress, a thief, and an ally in the calm, sensible blacksmith. With the help of the ghost, The Great Chaffalo, Touch discovers his great-uncle's villainous plot, saves the damsel's inn, and recovers his own inheritance.

Introducing the Book
Read aloud the first chapter to give potential readers an excellent start on this quickly moving story. The elements of a ghost story and a tall tale with gothic and romantic overtones are combined in this fantasy-adventure guaranteed to please readers of all ages.

Booktalks

In the Aisle
The Midnight Horse includes an orphan, an evil uncle, a ghost, a thief, a damsel in distress, and a magician. Can Touch, the orphan, outsmart his nasty uncle and his plot to rule the village? How can a friendly magician ghost help Touch?

With the Author's Words

When Touch arrives in Cricklewood to look up his only relative, he discovers his great-uncle is the town judge and the town grouch and is trying to swindle Touch out of his inheritance.

> *Anger was blazing up inside Touch. His great-uncle was not only a cunning rascal, but a miser. "Keep the confounded thirty-seven cents, same as everything else my pa left...." The judge glared. "Sign for what's yours!" ... "I don't choose to put my name to anything." "Don't cross me, Nephew," warned the judge. "Put your name to this document, or I'll scratch out another! I'll commit you to the orphan house!" "You'll have to catch me first."* (Pp. 26-27, hardback edition)

Outsmarting his crafty uncle is Touch's only hope to avoid being sent to an orphanage. Touch thinks he might have a chance when he is befriended by a ghost who magically produces *The Midnight Horse*.

Literature Extensions/Alternative Book Report Activities

Art—The illustrator, Peter Sis, uses the stipple technique in his artwork. This method of painting, drawing, or engraving uses small dots instead of lines or strokes. Each chapter in *The Midnight Horse* begins with a small illustration that foreshadows events. Students can use the stipple technique to illustrate each chapter's end.

Drama—*The Midnight Horse* is an excellent example of melodrama. Students can script this novel using the sensational, suspenseful style provided by Fleischman. Stage this play in true melodramatic style with a minimum of props, utilizing the bold characterizations and emotional dialogue.

Language Arts—Refer to the paragraph on page 80 (hardback edition) concerning the letter to Touch from his father: "The letter embraced him like strong arms." Students can write their own versions of what they think the letter might have said.

Literature—The thief, Otis Cratt, thinks he is invisible and parades through town in full view of all the citizens. Like the emperor in Hans Christian Andersen's "The Emperor's New Clothes," Cratt eventually discovers he was fooled. Students can compare and contrast these events or write their own original stories illustrating this theme, or both.

Sid Fleischman Wrote:

By the Great Spoon

Chancy and the Grand Rascal

The Ghost in the Noon-day Sun

The Ghost on Saturday Night

The Hey Hey Man

Humbug Mountain

The Midnight Horse

Mr. Mysterious & Company

The Whipping Boy

If you loved *The Midnight Horse* by Sid Fleischman, you'll like:

Babbitt, Natalie. *The Devil's Other Storybook*

———. *The Devil's Storybook*

Brittain, Bill. *Dr. Dredd's Wagon of Wonders*

———. *The Wish Giver*

Dahl, Roald. *Matilda*

Levoy, Myron. *The Magic Hat of Mortimer Wintergreen*

Pullman, Philip. *Spring-Heeled Jack*

Be a Magician

Barry, Sheila Anne. *Tricks & Stunts to Fool Your Friends*

Cobb, Vicki. *Magic ... Naturally! Science Entertainments and Amusements*

Day, Jon. *Let's Make Magic*

Friedhoffer, Robert. *Magic Tricks, Science Facts*

———. *More Magic Tricks, Science Facts*

Lewis, Shari, and Abraham B. Hurwitz. *Magic for Non-Magicians*

Severn, Bill. *More Magic in Your Pockets*

Tarr, Bill. *Now You See It, Now You Don't! Lessons in Sleight of Hand*

Townsend, Charles Barry. *World's Best Magic Tricks*

Fritz, Jean
Bully for You, Teddy Roosevelt!

LC 90-8142, ©1991, 127p., $15.95 (ISBN 0-399-21769-X), Putnam

Genres: Nonfiction, biography

Themes: Teddy Roosevelt, family life, fathers and sons, overcoming illness, natural history, cowboys, politics, war, presidency, courage, perseverance

Reading level: Sixth grade

Interest level: Fifth through ninth grades

Reviews:
Booklist. 87(16):1638 April 15, 1991
Bulletin of the Center for Children's Books. 44(9):216-17 May, 1991. (Recommended)
Horn Book. 67(4):476-77 July/August, 1991. (Starred)
School Library Journal. 37(7):79 July, 1991. (Starred)
Voice of Youth Advocates. 14(3):188 August, 1991. (#4 quality, #4 popularity)

Author Information

Jean Fritz was born in Hankow, China, in 1915. She lived there until she came to America with her parents in 1927. Completing her education in the United States, Fritz graduated from Wheaton College and attended Columbia University. Having been a research assistant, children's librarian, teacher, and book reviewer, it seemed natural for Fritz to turn to writing. Well-known for her historical fiction, Fritz often uses family stories for inspiration. The story of her childhood is recounted in her autobiography *Homesick: My Own Story* (Putnam, 1982) and her book *China Homecoming* (Putnam, 1985).

Plot Summary

This is an account of the life of Teddy Roosevelt from his sickly boyhood to his boisterous presidency. Roosevelt's personality is revealed through his interest in natural history, politics, the West, and sports. His legacy is the result of his achievements with the Rough Riders and the war in Cuba, the development of the Panama Canal, and the creation of the National Parks system.

Introducing the Book

Present this book by reading aloud pages 9-10 (hardback edition), ending with "would ever grow up at all." This biography reads like a novel because of the exciting presentation of Roosevelt's life. There's plenty of action and adventure. Consider introducing this book in celebration of President's Day.

Booktalks

In the Aisle

Did you ever wonder how the teddy bear got its name? Would you believe it was named after a president? It's true. And you can read about this Teddy in Jean Fritz's *Bully for You, Teddy Roosevelt!*

With the Author's Words

Teddy Roosevelt once asked a friend if the public minded when he tramped through the local parks in a slouch hat and top boots.

> *"You must not forget," the friend replied, "that you are the president...." Roosevelt argued that when he was acting as president, he too was dignified. "But Mr. President," the friend pointed out, "you are the president all the time." He was also Theodore Roosevelt all the time. And he decided that he was not going to change his habits even if he was president. (P. 103, hardback edition)*

Teddy Roosevelt's habits make him one of the most fascinating and down-to-earth presidents ever to live in the White House. This book has interesting facts never found in most history books. When you read it, you'll think *Bully for You, Teddy Roosevelt!*

Literature Extensions/Alternative Book Report Activities

American History—Along with Fritz's biography of Teddy Roosevelt, provide students with the excellent *Theodore Roosevelt Takes Charge* by Nancy Whitelaw (Whitman, 1992). The two books differ in text and tone, offering students an opportunity to contrast the two biographical styles. Fritz's book focuses on Roosevelt's exuberant personality, and Whitelaw concentrates on the nearly unbelievable accomplishments that were the result of Roosevelt's strong personality.

A related video is *American Portraits: Theodore Roosevelt—The Cowboy President* (American Heritage Productions).

Geography/National Parks and Monuments—Provide students with a list of national parks and monuments along with the addresses. Students can select a park or monument to write to and request visitor's information. Materials received can be shared in oral presentations, bulletin board displays, and so on.

Science/Conservation/Environment—Roosevelt was responsible for the beginnings of the conservation movement. He worked to save forests and wildlife by establishing 150 national forests, fifty-five bird and game preserves, eighteen national monuments, and five national parks. Roosevelt's nationwide system of wildlife refuges is explained in Dorothy Hinshaw Patent's *Places of Refuge: Our National Wildlife Refuge System* (Clarion Books, 1992). This legacy was left to all of us. Students in your class can continue the conservation movement by becoming more environmentally aware.

Provide students with some of the many recent books about what they can do in their communities for the environment. These include *The Future for the Environment* by Mark Lambert (Franklin Watts, 1986), *Save the Earth: An Action Handbook for Kids* by Betty Miles (Alfred A. Knopf, 1990), *50 Simple Things Kids Can Do to Save the Earth* (Andrews and McNeel, 1990), *Earth Book for Kids: Activities to Help Heal the Environment* by Linda Schwartz (Learning Works, 1990), *Our World* by Gayle Bittinger (Warren, 1990), *Earth Day Every Day* by Jill C. Wheeler (Abdo & Daughters, 1991), *Earth Day* by Linda Lowery (Carolrhoda Books, 1991), *Keepers of the Earth* by Michael J. Caduto and Joseph Bruchac (Fulcrum, 1989), and *Going Green: A Kid's Handbook to Saving the Planet* by John Elking (Viking, 1990). An annotated reference guide to environmental books for children is *E for Environment: An Annotated Bibliography of Children's Books with Environmental Themes* by Patti K. Sinclair (R. R. Bowker, 1992).

Students can develop a "going green" project either individually or as a class. Contact Kids for Saving Earth, P.O. Box 27247, Plymouth, MN 55447, to find out about forming a "Kids for Saving Earth" (KSE) club in your school or community. You can also write to Kids Against Pollution, P.O. Box 775, Closter, NJ 07624, to discover what other students are doing about pollution.

Science/Natural History—As a boy, Roosevelt created his own natural history museum—"The Roosevelt Museum of Natural History." Create a natural history museum in your classroom with everyone making contributions and explanations. If a natural history museum is located in your area, plan a class field trip for a look or invite a docent to visit your class with handouts and sample displays. For reading material consult *A Practical Guide for the Amateur Naturalist* by Gerald Durrell (Alfred A. Knopf, 1982).

Jean Fritz Wrote:

Brady

Bully for You, Teddy Roosevelt!

The Cabin Faced West

Champion Dog Prince Tom

China Homecoming

China's Long March

The Double Life of Pocahontas

Early Thunder

The Great Little Madison

Homesick: My Own Story

Make Way for Sam Houston

Traitor, the Case of Benedict Arnold

Cowboys

Ashabranner, Brent. *Born to the Land: An American Portrait*

Freedman, Russell. *Cowboys of the Wild West*

Fritz, Jean. *Bully for You, Teddy Roosevelt!*

Martini, Terry. *Cowboys*

Matthews, Leonard J. *Cowboys*

Rounds, Glenn. *Cowboys*

Ward, Don. *Cowboys and Cattle Country*

Wolf, Bernard. *Cowboy*

American Presidents

Freedman, Russell. *Lincoln: A Photobiography*

Fritz, Jean. *Bully for You, Teddy Roosevelt!*

———. *The Great Little Madison*

Greenberg, Morrie. *The Buck Stops Here: A Biography of Harry Truman*

Harrison, Barbara, and Daniel Terris. *A Twilight Struggle: The Life of John Fitzgerald Kennedy*

Meltzer, Milton. *George Washington and the Birth of Our Nation*

Hoover, H. M.
Away Is a Strange Place to Be

LC 89-34455, ©1990, 167p., $14.95 (ISBN 0-525-44505-6), Dutton Children's Books

Genres: Science fiction, adventure

Themes: Slave labor, kidnapping, fear, artificial worlds, space travel, cooperation, construction, courage, independence, selfishness, escape, friendship, love, anger, individuality

Reading level: Fifth grade

Interest level: Fifth through eighth grades

Reviews:
Booklist. 86(7):743-44 December 1, 1989
Bulletin of the Center for Children's Books.
    43(6):139 February, 1990. (Recommended)
School Library Journal. 36(1):104 January, 1990
Voice of Youth Advocates. 12(6):371 February,
    1990. (#5 quality, #4 popularity)

Author Information
H. M. (Helen Mary) Hoover grew up in a book-loving family and learned to read at the age of four. As a child she read anything and everything. Hoover attended nursing school but soon discovered nursing was not the career for her. At the age of thirty-two, she says, she decided "it might be nice to write." So Hoover quit her job and spent four years learning the craft of writing. Since then she has averaged about a book per year. For Hoover, writing is sometimes fun and sometimes not. She writes to please herself and hopes that what pleases and interests her will appeal to others.

Plot Summary
Twelve-year-olds Abby, from Earth, and spoiled, rich Bryan, a colonial from Triark, are kidnapped and taken to the planet VitaCon to work in labor gangs building an artificial habitat. Abby resists captivity because her life on Earth was filled with love and her uncle encouraged her to be independent. Many of the other captive children seem satisfied with their lot, but not Bryan. Reluctantly feeling responsible for Bryan, Abby risks her own escape by including him.

Introducing the Book
This fast-paced adventure will appeal even to readers who normally do not select science fiction. The perennially favorite theme of kids outwitting adults and surviving on their own will make this an easy sell. Read aloud to page 21 (hardback edition) to "she saw the man was gaining on them."

Booktalks

In the Aisle
When twelve-year-old Abby is kidnapped and taken to a distant planet to work as a slave, all she can think about is escaping. She's smart enough to do it on her own but feels responsible for helping Bryan, the spoiled brat who insists on coming along. Can they make it together?

With the Author's Words
Abby's dream seems very peculiar. Loud voices are shouting orders and she's unsure of where she is.

> She was lying in a plastic jar with big round holes in the sides ... she was covered by soft mesh. All around her were rows of identical jars ... in each jar was a person her age or younger. There was a girl in the jar to her right, a boy on the left. She looked more closely at the boy. It was Bryan. Somehow it was fitting that he should be in her nightmare. (P. 2, hardback edition)

Why would Bryan show up in Abby's dream when she's tried every way she can to avoid him in real life? But this isn't a dream, and Abby discovers that *Away Is* (definitely) *a Strange Place to Be.*

Literature Extensions/Alternative Book Report Activities

Art/Architecture—Design, draw, or build the artificial colony on VitaCon as described on pages 44-46, hardback edition. Provide students with architectural materials such as *Fun with Architecture* by David Eisen (Metropolitan Museum of Art, 1992). This kit of rubber stamps and an instructional booklet allow recreations of architectural masterpieces or the creation of imaginary buildings.

Other books on the basics of architecture include *Incredible Cross-Sections* by Richard Pratt (Alfred A. Knopf, 1992); David Macaulay's *Unbuilding* (Houghton Mifflin, 1980), *City: A Story of Roman Planning and Construction* (Houghton Mifflin, 1974), and *Castle* (Houghton Mifflin, 1977); and *Grand Constructions* by Gian Paolo Ceserani and Piero Ventura (Putnam, 1983).

Science—Students can more readily understand the intricacies involved in establishing an artificial habitat like VitaCon by looking at the Biosphere 2 project in Arizona. Research the construction, operation, and success of Biosphere 2 through newspapers and periodicals. Related books include *The Glass Ark: The Story of the Biosphere 2* by Linnea Geutry (Viking, 1991) and *Biosphere 2: The Human Experiment* by John Allen (Viking, 1991).

Science/Space Travel—One of the appeals of reading science fiction is the realization that mankind will colonize space in the future. The reality of space station development is at its early stages.

Interested students can consult the following books for further information about the United States' space program (the National Aeronautics and Space Administration, or NASA) and future homes in space: *Space, Stars, Planets, and Spacecraft* by Sue Becklack (Dorling Kindersley, 1991), *Space Enterprise: Beyond NASA* by David Gump (Praeger, 1990), *Pioneering Space* by Sandra Markle (Atheneum, 1992), *Daring the Unknown: A History of NASA* by Howard Everett Smith (Harcourt Brace Jovanovich, 1987), *The Space Station* by Kent Alexander (Gallery Books, 1988), *Colonizing the Planets and Stars* by Isaac Asimov (Gareth Stevens, 1990), *Lunar Bases* by Shaaron Cosner (Franklin Watts, 1990), *Welcome to Moonbase* by Ben Bova (Ballantine Books, 1987), *Living in Space* by James S. Trefil (Scribner, 1981), and *Homes in Space* by Graham Rickard (Lerner, 1989).

Sociology/Child Labor—In Hoover's novell children throughout the solar system were being kidnapped to work as slaves for a construction company despite laws protecting children. Throughout history, children have been exploited and used for financial gain.

Students can look at the history of the development of child labor laws by referring to books such as *Child Labor: Then and Now* by Laura Offenhartz Green (Franklin Watts, 1992). Fictional accounts like Katherine Paterson's *Lyddie* (Lodestar, 1991), and *The Clock* by James Lincoln Collier and Christopher Collier (Delacorte Press, 1992) can help to explain why legislation was necessary in order to protect children.

H. M. Hoover Wrote:

Another Heaven, Another Earth

Away Is a Strange Place to Be

The Bell Tree

Children of Morrow

The Dawn Palace

The Delikon

The Lost Star

Only Child

Orvis

Return to Earth: A Novel of the Future

The Shepherd Moon: A Novel of the Future

The Time of Darkness

Future Lives, Distant Places

Asimov, Isaac, et al. eds. *Young Star Travelers*

Christopher, John. *The Dragon Dance Trilogy*

Hill, Douglas. *Exiles of ColSec*

Hoover, H.M. *Away Is a Strange Place to Be*

Karl, Jean. *But We Are Not of Earth*

Norton, Andre. *Star Gate*

Pinkwater, Daniel. *Alan Mendelsohn, the Boy from Mars*

Sargent, Pamela. *Earthseed*

SF - F = F (Science Fiction Minus Fiction Equals the Future)

Caraker, Mary. *The Faces of Ceti*

Christopher, John. *The White Mountain Quartet*

Hill, Douglas. *Alien Citadel*

Hoover, H. M. *Away Is a Strange Place to Be*

Hughes, Monica. *Devil on My Back*

Karl, Jean. *Strange Tomorrow*

Lawrence, Louise. *Calling B for Butterfly*

O'Brien, Robert Conly. *Z for Zachariah*

Sargent, Pamela. *Alien Child*

Service, Pamela F. *Under Alien Stars*

Sleator, William. *Green Futures of Tycho*

——. *Interstellar Pig*

Yolen, Jane. *The Pit Dragon Trilogy*

Koller, Jackie French
If I Had One Wish...

LC 91-9013, ©1991, 161p., $14.95 (ISBN 0-316-501150-6), Little, Brown

Genres: Contemporary realistic fiction, fantasy

Themes: Brothers, love, family life, responsibility, wishes, magic, dreams, kindness, truthfulness, self-discovery, the homeless, basketball

Reading level: Fourth grade

Interest level: Fifth through eighth grades

Reviews:
Booklist. 88(5):506 November 1, 1991
Bulletin of the Center for Children's Books. 45(4):96 December, 1991
School Library Journal. 37(11):120 November, 1991

Author Information
Jackie French Koller loves magic and make-believe and considers books her natural companions. As a child she was quiet and shy, preferring to watch, listen, and pretend. Her school experiences with reading were dismal, but later, in reading aloud to her own children, Koller discovered the joy to be found in books. She says, "My long-slumbering imagination came vividly alive and I found my life's vocation—writing books." As is the case with many authors, it took years of receiving rejection slips before Koller was finally published. Now she says it is difficult to supply the demand. Koller and her husband live with their three children in Groton, Massachusetts. *If I Had One Wish...* was inspired by her children.

Plot Summary
Six-foot-two Alec, an eighth-grader nicknamed "Giraffe," is struggling with his adolescence. He tries to cope with girls, sports, a demanding father, a talented older sister, and an obnoxious and adoring younger brother, Stevie. When Alec helps an elderly woman, she insists he take what she calls a magic talisman. Surprisingly, the magic works and a careless wish deletes Stevie from the family. Alec is the only person who knows that Stevie ever existed. The realization of Stevie's importance to the family drives Alec to find the old woman and take back his wish.

Introducing the Book
This book was selected for the ALA/YALSA Recommended Books for Reluctant Young Adult Readers 1992 booklist. Introduce it by using the booktalks listed below or read aloud the first chapter in order to hook potential readers.

Booktalks

In the Aisle
If you had an irritating little brother, one who really drove you crazy, and a magic, wish-granting coin, what would you do? In this book, Alec makes a disastrous wish that changes his life—and his family's.

In the Author's Words

> [The elderly woman] leaned against him secretly and tried to press a coin into his hand. Alec pushed it back. "No, no," he said. "I don't want any money." ... "It is a talisman," said the old woman. "A talisman?" Alec repeated. The old woman nodded gravely. "It will give you one wish," she whispered. "Use it with care." (P. 30, hardback edition)

Now you know why this book by Jackie French Koller is called *If I Had One Wish....* What you don't know is, how careful will Alec be?

Literature Extensions/Alternative Book Report Activities

Creative Writing—If you had a wish, what would you wish for? What would happen if it really came true? Students can write their own wishes and results, along with the responsibilities that seem to go along with having one's wishes come true.

Current Events/The Homeless—Abbey works at a soup kitchen and is very concerned about the homeless. Use this book as a springboard for a study of the homeless issue. Writing projects can be based on research from periodicals, newspapers, and television news reports and should include information on the homeless in your community. Students may write about this issue, create suggestions for assistance, interview local officials, volunteer at a soup kitchen, encourage schools to donate leftover cafeteria food to local shelters, and so on.

Useful books are Jonathan Kozol's *Rachel and Her Children: Homeless Families in America* (Crown, 1988), *No Place to Be: Voices of Homeless Children* by Judith Berck (Houghton, 1992), *The Place I Call Home* by Lois Stavsky and I. E. Mozeson (Shapolsky, 1991), *Homeless in America* by Anna Kosof (Franklin Watts, 1988), and Margaret O. Hyde's *The Homeless: Profiling the Problem* (Enslow, 1989).

A collection of paintings, poems, and stories for younger children can be found in *Home* edited by Michael J. Rosen (HarperCollins, 1992). Proceeds from the sales of *Home* will be donated to Share Our Strength, a nonprofit organization that provides funds for aid to people who are homeless. For further information students can write to the National Coalition for the Homeless, 311 South Spring Street, Los Angeles, CA 90013.

Film—The classic Frank Capra movie *It's a Wonderful Life* (RKO, 1946) reflects on the importance of the individual. On a similar note, Alec realizes that his family's life is drastically different, and not so wonderful without Stevie. Provide the film for classroom viewing or announce its television showing and invite discussion or essays or both on this theme.

Language Arts/Art—Write or illustrate a story or episode about "the Wanderer, Yohilda," and what her life is like. She says, "It is a Wanderer's lot to live on the kindness of others, rewarding that kindness" (P. 130, hardback edition).

The Homeless

Corcoran, Barbara. *Stay Tuned*

Fox, Paula. *Monkey Island*

Greenberg, Keith Elliot. *Erik Is Homeless*

Hahn, Mary Downing. *December Stillness*

Holman, Felice. *Secret City USA*

——. *Slake's Limbo*

Hughes, Dean. *Family Pose*

Koller, Jackie French. *If I Had One Wish...*

Paulsen, Gary. *The Crossing*

Sachs, Marilyn. *At the Sound of the Beep*

Spinelli, Jerry. *Maniac Magee*

Wojciechowski, Susan. *Patty Dillman of Hot Dog Fame*

Oh, Brother!

Adler, David. *Ghost Brother*

Blume, Judy. *Fudge-A-Mania*

——. *Superfudge*

Byars, Betsy. *Bingo Brown, Gypsy Lover*

Getz, David. *Thin Air*

Hobbs, Will. *The Big Wander*

Koller, Jackie French. *If I Had One Wish...*

Levinson, Marilyn. *And Don't Bring Jeremy*

Martin, Ann M. *Inside Out*

Roberts, Willo Davis. *Scared Stiff*

Schwartz, Joel L. *How to Get Rid of Your Older Brother*

Wishes

Banks, Lynn Reid. *The Fairy Rebel*

Brittain, Bill. *The Wish Giver*

Catling, Patrick. *The Chocolate Touch*

Conford, Ellen. *Genie with the Light Blue Hair*

Dexter, Catherine. *Gertie's Green Thumb*

Eager, Edgar. *Half-Magic*

Hutchins, H. J. *The Three and Many Wishes of Jason Reid*

Koller, Jackie French. *If I Had One Wish...*

Sargent, Sarah. *Jonas McFee, A.T.P.*

Sterman, Betsy, and Samuel Sterman. *Too Much Magic*

York, Carol Beach. *Miss Know It All and the Wishing Lamp*

O'Dell, Scott, and Elizabeth Hall
Thunder Rolling in the Mountains

LC 91-15961, ©1992, 128p., $14.95 (ISBN 0-395-59966-0), Houghton Mifflin

Genre: Historical fiction, multicultural

Themes: American Indians-Nez Perce, self-determination, courage, battles, independence, cruelty, heroism, trust, family, love, romance, death, reservations, treaties, peace, revenge

Reading level: Fifth grade

Interest level: Fifth through ninth grades

Reviews:
Booklist. 88(20):1834 June 15, 1992. (Starred)
Bulletin of the Center for Children's Books. 45(8):218 April, 1992. (Recommended)
Horn Book. 68(2):205 March/April 1992
School Library Journal. 38(8):156 August, 1992
Voice of Youth Advocates. 15(1):34 April, 1992. (#5 quality, #3 popularity)

Author Information

Born in 1903 in Los Angeles, Scott O'Dell attended Occidental College, the University of Wisconsin, Stanford University, and the University of Rome. In 1934 O'Dell began full-time writing, following stints as a cameraman and a book editor for a Los Angeles newspaper. His first children's book was *Island of the Blue Dolphins* (Houghton Mifflin, 1960), which won the Newbery Award; he was a three-time Newbery Honor Book winner. O'Dell preferred writing for children, finding it fun and rewarding. However, he believed his books were not strictly for children. "In one sense," he said, "they were written for myself, out of happy and unhappy memories and a personal need." Available from Houghton Mifflin is a videotape called "A Visit With Scott O'Dell."

O'Dell died in October, 1989, midway through the writing of *Thunder Rolling in the Mountains*. His wife, Elizabeth Hall, had participated in the development of the manuscript. This included travel along the Nez Perce trail, reading, research, and constant discussions about characters and events in the story. An experienced writer and editor, Hall has published fiction and nonfiction for readers of all ages. Her collaboration with O'Dell, particularly with this book, enabled her to complete the manuscript with O'Dell's style and spirit intact.

Plot Summary

Fourteen-year-old Sound of Running Feet, daughter of Chief Joseph of the Nez Perce Indians, tells the story of the forced removal of the Nez Perce from their homeland. They retreat to northern Montana in an effort to avoid reservation life. While being pursued by U.S. soldiers, the tribal chiefs disagree on their course of action and fight battles with the soldiers and their allies. Huge losses are suffered before the Nez Perce surrender and Sound of Running Feet escapes.

Introducing the Book

The book fairly zooms through twenty-three chapters plus a foreword and afterword. Reading aloud the first couple of chapters will be sufficient to launch the action. This book tells of the events of 1877, when Chief Joseph and his people were driven from their homeland by the U.S. soldiers.

Booktalks

In the Aisle

Thunder Rolling in the Mountains is the story of the Nez Perce Indians' last year of freedom as they try to avoid being forced to live on a reservation. Bloody battles and bitter betrayals mark their tragic flight north. With bravery and determination the Nez Perce make a last stand.

With the Authors' Words

Sound of Running Feet retells an argument between her father, Chief Joseph, and General Howard of the U.S. Army.

> The general pointed a glittering sword at my father. "Listen," he shouted. "I have heard enough excuses. Now I speak my last words. If you have not moved your tribe from this place before thirty suns have risen and set, then I shall send soldiers with guns to drive you out." (P. 16, hardback edition)

What Howard really wants is the valuable land that the Nez Perce have lived on for generations. Many want to stay and face the soldiers with guns, but Chief Joseph fears for his people, and he has only thirty days to decide what to do.

Literature Extensions/Alternative Book Report Activities

Communications/Telegraph—The Nez Perce realize that the U.S. soldiers can communicate in a fast and seemingly magical manner by using the "click clack." The invention of the telegraph played an important role in western migration and development.

Students interested in learning more can refer to *Communications* by Trevor Fisher (Batsford, 1985), *Communications* by Ian Graham (Hamstead, 1989), *Wires West* by Philip H. Ault (Dodd Mead, 1974), *Morse, Marconi, and You* by Irwin Math (Scribner, 1979), and *Marconi, Father of Radio* by David Gunston (Crowell-Collier, 1965).

Geology/Yellowstone National Park—While fleeing the U.S. soldiers, the Nez Perce tribe spend some time in what is now Yellowstone National Park. Sound of Running Feet comments on the hot springs they swim in.

Interested students can learn more about this park and other natural hot springs by referring to *Letting Off Steam: The Story of Geothermal Energy* by Linda Jacobs (Carolrhoda Books, 1989), *The Hiker's Guide to Hotsprings in the Pacific Northwest* by Evi Litton (Falcon Press, 1990), *The Geysers of Yellowstone* by T. Scott Bryan (Colorado Associated University Press, 1986), and *Roadside Geology of the Yellowstone Country* by William J. Fritz (Mountain Press, 1985).

History/Indians—*Thunder Rolling in the Mountains* is based on real events occurring in 1877 as the Nez Perce were driven from their homeland. Nonfiction materials with information about this time include Russell Freedman's *Indian Chiefs* (Holiday House, 1987) and *An Indian Winter* (Holiday House, 1992), *A Final Promise: The Campaign to Assimilate the Indians 1880-1920* by Frederick Hoxie (University of Nebraska Press, 1974), *Indian Country* by Peter Matthiessen (Viking, 1984), *The Indians of Yellowstone Park* by Joel C. Janetski (University of Utah Press, 1987), and *The Dispossession of the American Indian, 1887-1934* by Janet A. Mcdonnell (Indiana University Press, 1991).

For specific information about Chief Joseph and the Nez Perce Indians, consult *The Nez Perce* by Clifford E. Trafzer (Chelsea, 1992), *Chief Joseph: Thunder Rolling from the Mountains* by Diana Yates (Ward Hill, 1992), and *Chief Joseph of the Nez Perce Indians: Champion of Liberty* by M. Fox (Childrens Press, 1992).

Storytelling—The oral tradition of storytelling was essential to the Nez Perce for entertainment as well as passing along cultural mores and traditions. It is exemplified by the telling of the Coyote stories on page 49. Students can easily learn this important art form. Caroline Feller Bauer's *Read for the Fun of It: Active Programming with Books for Children* (H. W. Wilson, 1992) includes a chapter titled "Teaching Children to Tell Stories." Not only is it filled with instructions on getting started, the development of techniques, and stories to tell, but also includes an extensive listing of stories from collections and picture books appropriate for children to tell.

Other valuable resources include Norma J. Livo and Sandra A. Rietz's *Storytelling Folklore Sourcebook* (Libraries Unlimited, 1991) and *Storytelling: Process and Practice* (Libraries Unlimited, 1986), as well as *Twice Upon a Time: Stories to Tell, Retell, Act Out and Write About* by Judy Sierra and Robert Kaminski (H. W. Wilson, 1989). For specific Native American tales, consult *American Indian Myths and Legends* selected and edited by Richard Erdoes and Alfonso Ortiz (Pantheon Books, 1984) and *Literatures of the American Indian* by A. Lavonne Brown Ruoff (Chelsea House, 1991).

Scott O'Dell Wrote:

Alexandra

Black Star, Bright Dawn

The Captive

The Castle in the Sea

Island of the Blue Dolphins

My Name Is Not Angelica

The Road to Damietta

The Serpent Never Sleeps: A Novel of Jamestown and Pocahontas

Streams to the River, River to the Sea: A Novel of Sacagawea

Westward Expansion

Blumberg, Rhoda. The Incredible Journey of Lewis and Clark

Freedman, Russell. Buffalo Hunt

——. Children of the Wild West

——. Indian Chiefs

Hanmer, Trudy J. The Advancing Frontier

Marrin, Albert. War Clouds in the West: Indians and Cavalrymen, 1860-1890

Reynolds, Quentin. Custer's Last Stand

Indian Girls: Tales of the Past

Dorris, Michael. Morning Girl

Gregory, Kristiana. Jenny of the Tetons

Highwater, Jamake. Legend Days

Hudson, Jan. Dawn Rider

——. Sweetgrass

Meyer, Carolyn. Where the Broken Heart Still Beats

O'Dell, Scott. Black Star, Bright Dawn

——. The Serpent Never Sleeps: A Novel of Jamestown and Pocahontas

——. Streams to the River, River to the Sea: A Novel of Sacagawea

O'Dell, Scott, and Elizabeth Hall. Thunder Rolling in the Mountains

Root, Phyllis. The Listening Silence

Spinka, Penina Keen. Mother's Blessing

——. White Hare's Horses

Thomasma, Ken. Naya Nuki

——. Pathki Nana: Kootnai Girl

Paulsen, Gary
Woodsong

LC 89-70835, ©1990, 132p., $12.95 (ISBN 0-02-770221-9), Bradbury Press. Paperback $3.95 (ISBN 0-14-034905-8), Puffin Books

Genres: Biography, adventure

Themes: Wilderness, sled dogs, man against nature, survival, animal behavior, respect, danger, beauty, accidents, the Iditarod race, trapping

Reading level: Fifth grade

Interest level: Sixth grade and up

Reviews:
Booklist. 88(22):2164 August, 1990
Bulletin of the Center for Children's Books. 44(2):41 October, 1990. (Recommended)
Horn Book. 66(6):762 November/December, 1990
School Library Journal. 36(10):148 October, 1991. (Starred)
Voice of Youth Advocates. 13(5):318 December, 1990. (#4 quality, #3 popularity)

Author Information

Gary Paulsen has tried many careers but always comes back to writing. Born in Minnesota, Paulsen is a second-generation American with a Scandinavian background. As a child of a career military father, he moved around constantly, never living for more than five months in one spot. His childhood was not happy; he had no friends, didn't do well in sports, and wasn't very successful in school. While in high school, he discovered the public library and read voraciously. After four years in the U.S. Army, Paulsen went to work in the aerospace industry. When he discovered he had writing talent, he left his job and became an editor and writer. He has written extensively—more than 200 short stories, articles, plays, novels, and nonfiction works. Dividing his time between New Mexico and Wyoming, Paulsen continues to research his writing by experiencing everything firsthand. His wife, Ruth Wright Paulsen, is an artist and made the photograph of Paulsen and his dog that appears on the cover of *Woodsong*. Paulsen says the publisher loved the photograph because it looks as if the dog is giving him a kiss. In reality, sled dogs take every opportunity to lick dripping noses—they love the salt!

Plot Summary

Focusing on his sled dogs and wildlife, writer Gary Paulsen shares recollections of his life in the Minnesota wilderness. As Paulsen describes various animal personalities, he relates his changing feelings regarding the wild. Using short entries he also details his running of the famed Iditarod dog sled race in Alaska with all its deprivations, excitement, and joy.

Introducing the Book

Select one or two of the following to read aloud: chapter 1, chapter 5, or portions of chapter 6. This book is especially appropriate to introduce in March when the Iditarod race takes place. Watch for current news stories in newspapers and magazines and on television. *Woodsong* was included on the ALA/YALSA's Recommended Books for the Reluctant Young Adult Reader list in 1991.

Booktalks

In the Aisle

Paulsen tells you what really happened to him when training his sled dogs and running his first Iditarod race in Alaska. He shares details about the fascinating personalities and quirks of his animals and his own growing respect for the wilderness and all things wild.

With the Author's Words
Paulsen is irritated when a marauding bear paws through his burning trash.

> *I was standing across the burning fire from him and without thinking—because I was so used to him—I picked up a stick, threw it at him, and yelled, "Get out of here." I have made many mistakes in my life, and will probably make many more, but I hope never to throw a stick at a bear again.* (P. 40, hardback and paperback editions)

Why was this a mistake? You'll have to read Gary Paulsen's true story, *Woodsong*.

Literature Extensions/Alternative Book Report Activities

Language Arts—*Woodsong* is an autobiographical account of a period in Paulsen's life. Allow students the opportunity to construct their own life stories, focusing on their individual family traditions, cultural backgrounds, and experiences. The books should reflect their past and its contribution to their current lives, describing each student's individuality. Use of mementos, photographs, and other writings should be encouraged. For an excellent example, see *War Boy: A Country Childhood* (Arcade, 1990), the illustrated autobiography of Michael Foreman.

Science/Animal Behavior—Paulsen spent years training his dogs for the Iditarod. Students can learn the basics of dog training and dogs' underlying behavior by consulting Desmond Morris's *Dogwatching* (Crown, 1986), *Dog Training for Kids* by Carol Lea Benjamin (Howell, 1988), *Understanding Man's Best Friend: Why Dogs Look and Act the Way They Do* by Ann Squire (Macmillan, 1991), and Jean Craighead George's *How to Talk to Your Dog* (Warner Books, 1985).

Science/Wildlife—Paulsen writes fascinating accounts of his animal observations. Every aspect is of interest to him, including various animal characteristics, tracks, behavior, and so on.
For interested students provide the following books for further information about the intriguing world of animals: *Secrets of a Wildlife Watcher* by Jim Arnosky (Lothrop, Lee & Shepard, 1983), *How Animals Behave: A New Look at Wildlife* edited by Donald J. Crump (National Geographic Society, 1984), *How Smart Are Animals?* by Dorothy Hinshaw Patent (Harcourt Brace Jovanovich, 1990), *Animal Talk* by Karen Gravelle and Ann Squire (Messner, 1988), *Crusade of a Northwoods Veterinarian* by Dr. Rory C. Foster (Franklin Watts, 1985), and *A Field Guide to Animal Tracks* by Olaus J. Murie (Houghton Mifflin, 1974).
A related computer software program is *Animal Trackers* (Wings for Learning/Sunburst), which offers trackers a choice of three habitats as well as three levels of difficulty.

Sports/History—The Iditarod race is run every year between Anchorage and Nome, Alaska, in celebration of the historic dog sled run which delivered needed serum to Nome in 1925. The race is named after a ghost town located along the trail. Montana's "Race to the Sky" is a 500-mile sled dog race that has been run since 1985. It is second only to the Iditarod.
Make available *Race Across Alaska: First Woman to Win the Iditarod Tells Her Story* by Libby Riddles and Tim Jones (Stackpole Books, 1988). For further information about this sport, refer to *Sled Dogs* by Brigid Casey and Wendy Haugh (Dodd, Mead, 1983). This book presents information about the history of the dogs, sledding, and dog sleds as a form of transportation.

Gary Paulsen Wrote:

Clabbered Dirt, Sweet Grass

Cookcamp

Dancing Carl

Dogsong

Hatchet

Haymeadow

Murphy

Nightjohn

Sentries

Tracker

The Voyage of the Frog

Woodsong

Animals and Adventure

Burgess, Melvin. *The Cry of the Wolf*

George, Jean Craighead. *Julie of the Wolves*

Houston, James. *Frozen Fire: A Tale of Courage*

Malterre, Elona. *The Last Wolf of Ireland*

Martin, Guenn. *Forty Miles from Nowhere: A Winter Adventure in Alaska*

North, Sterling. *The Wolfling*

Paulsen, Gary. *Dogsong*

———. *Woodsong*

Dog Sledding—Across the Snow and Ice

Calvert, Patricia. *The Hour of the Wolf*

Casey, Brigid, and Wendy Haugh. *Sled Dogs*

Gardiner, John. *Stone Fox*

O'Dell, Scott. *Black Star, Bright Dawn*

Paulsen, Gary. *Dogsong*

——— . *Woodsong*

Riddles, Libby, and Tim Jones. *Race Across Alaska: First Woman to Win the Iditarod Tells Her Story*

Rappaport, Doreen

Living Dangerously: American Women Who Risked Their Lives for Adventure

LC 90-28915, ©1991, 117p., $13.89 (ISBN 0-0-06-025108-5; ISBN 0-06-025109-3, library binding), HarperCollins

Genres: Nonfiction, biography, adventure

Themes: Women, exploration, determination, courage, risks, pilots, safaris, wildlife, mountain climbing, scuba diving, scientific investigation, anthropology

Reading level: Sixth grade

Interest level: Fourth through tenth grades

Reviews:
Booklist. 88(3):326 October 1, 1991
School Library Journal. 37(12):127 December, 1991
Voice of Youth Advocates. 14(5):340 December, 1991. (#3 quality, #3 popularity)

Author Information

Doreen Rappaport lives in New York City. She has written several children's books and has also created award-winning educational programs focusing on literature, music, and American history.

Plot Summary

Six courageous and often daring American women of the twentieth century are portrayed in biographical sketches. Their adventures include shooting Niagara Falls in a barrel, mountain climbing, pioneer stunt flying, wildlife exploring in Africa, scuba diving, and competing as a disabled athlete. The stories are reconstructed from firsthand accounts as well as newspaper and magazine articles. Included is a selected bibliography and an appendix on female adventurers.

Introducing the Book

Using a collective biography such as *Living Dangerously* is a great way to introduce biographies as a genre. Because the individual sketches are very short, reading aloud one or two selections will quickly give students a taste of the entire work. If any students are interested in a particular hobby detailed in this book, select that chapter.

Booktalks

In the Aisle

Have you ever wanted to go over Niagara Falls in a barrel? Or visit pygmies in Africa? Or climb a never-before-climbed mountain peak? These adventures and more are in *Living Dangerously* by Doreen Rappaport.

With the Author's Words

At the turn of the century, going over Niagara Falls in a barrel was appealing to many daredevils. Not all survived, and no woman had ever tried until October 25, 1901, when Annie Taylor climbed into a barrel.

> The barrel whirled away from the rocks, then whirled back and hit more rocks, and more rocks. Annie prayed her head wouldn't hit the top of the barrel. Faster, faster. The barrel gathered speed as it moved down the river.... Within four minutes the barrel reached the top of the falls. It paused a second, as if making up its mind whether or not to go, and then it plunged into the foaming falls. (P. 11, hardback edition)

Annie Taylor was truly an American woman who risked her life for adventure. Does she survive? Read *Living Dangerously* by Doreen Rappaport.

Literature Extensions/Alternative Book Report Activities

Art/Photography—Each adventurer is shown in at least one photograph in this book. All writing can be enhanced by the inclusion of photographs. Students, individually or in groups, may select a person or topic to write about, using photographs to extend the text.

Provide books illustrated with photographs such as Russell Freedman's *Lincoln: A Photobiography* (Ticknor and Fields, 1987) and *Cowboys of the Wild West* (Clarion Books, 1985), Jill Krementz's *How It Feels to Fight for Your Life* (Little, Brown, 1989), Patricia Lauber's *Volcano: The Eruption and Healing of Mount St. Helens* (Bradbury Press, 1986), and Kathryn Lasky and Christopher Knight's *Dinosaur Dig* (Morrow Junior Books, 1990).

Community Resources—Every community has adventurers who take risks and explore new territories. Even though they may not be the "first," these daring individuals can inspire others. Invite some of these people to your class to tell stories, show slides, set up displays, and so on. Consider this for an all-school assembly.

Physical Education/Physically Handicapped Athletes—Thecla Mitchell is a marathon racer who happens to be disabled and competes in a specially designed wheelchair. At the 1992 Summer Olympics, wheelchair racing was a demonstration sport. Numerous organizations and support groups for disabled athletes have been formed in recent years. Contact groups in your community that organize and sponsor events for disabled athletes. Students can volunteer their services and discover how rewarding this type of community service can be.

For further information consult *The Complete Directory for People With Disabilities* (Gale Research, 1992), *Move Over, Wheelchairs Coming Through: Seven Young People in Wheelchairs Talk About Their Lives* by Ron Roy (Clarion Books, 1985), and *Equal Rights for Americans with Disabilities* by Frank Bowe (Franklin Watts, 1992); or contact the U.S. Amputee Athletic Association, P.O. Box 15258, Colorado Springs, CO 80935, or the National Handicapped Sports and Recreation Association, 1145 19th Street, NW, Suite 717, Washington, DC 20036.

Science/Environment—In 1925, Delia Akeley was sent to the Belgian Congo (now Zaire) to study the animals and people for the Brooklyn Museum. A remote African rain forest near where Akeley explored has remained virtually untouched by humans. *Time* magazine featured this area in the cover story "The Last Eden" (July 13, 1992). Provide this article for a current accounting of an expedition in the Ndoki River region. The question is: Will this treasure be preserved? Interested students can pursue this with further research on this region and other remote areas.

Doreen Rappaport Wrote:

American Women: Their Lives in Their Words

The Boston Coffee Party

Escape From Slavery: Five Journeys to Freedom

Living Dangerously: America Women Who Risked Their Lives for Adventure

Trouble at the Mines

Real Women, Real Adventures

Archer, Jules. Breaking Barriers: The Feminist Revolution from Susan B. Anthony to Margaret Sanger to Betty Friedan

Ball, Jacqueline, and Catherine Conant. Georgia O'Keeffe: Painter of the Desert

Davidson, Sue. Getting the Real Story: Nelly Bly & Ida B. Wells

Faber, Doris. Calamity Jane: Her Life and Her Legend

Griffin, Lynne, and Kelly McCann. The Book of Woman: 300 Notable Women History Passed By

Lauber, Patricia. Lost Star: The Story of Amelia Earhart

Van Steenwyk, Elizabeth. Ida B. Wells-Barnett: Woman of Courage

Ward, Glenyse. Wandering Girl

Courageous Girls and Women—Fiction

Alexander, Lloyd. The Beggar Queen

Avi. The True Confessions of Charlotte Doyle

Cole, Sheila. Dragon in the Cliff

George, Jean Craighead. Julie of the Wolves

Gregory, Kristiana. Earthquake at Dawn

McCaffrey, Anne. Dragonsong

McKinley, Robin. Blue Sword

———. The Hero and the Crown

O'Dell, Scott. Island of the Blue Dolphins

Ross, Rhea Beth. The Bet's On, Lizzie Bingman!

Shore, Laura. Sacred Moon Tree

Strieber, Whitley. Wolf of Shadows

Service, Pamela F.
Being of Two Minds

LC 90-24097, ©1991, 169p., $13.95 (ISBN 0-689-31524-4), Atheneum. Paperback $3.99 (ISBN 0-449-70415-7), Fawcett Juniper

Genres: Mystery, science fiction, adventure, contemporary realistic fiction

Themes: Extrasensory perception, friendship, royalty, kidnapping, courage, treachery, neutrality, families

Reading level: Fifth grade

Interest level: Fifth through tenth grades

Reviews:
Booklist. 88(5):521 November 1, 1991
Bulletin of the Center for Children's Books.
    45(3):74 November, 1991. (Recommended)
School Library Journal. 37(10):128 October, 1991
Voice of Youth Advocates. 14(6):387 February, 1992. (#3 quality, #3 popularity)

Author Information

Pamela F. Service grew up loving science fiction and watching every science fiction movie she possibly could. Raised in Berkeley, California, Service also became interested in politics and archaeology. She graduated from the University of California at Berkeley in 1967 with a bachelor of arts degree in political science and later received a master of arts degree in African studies from the University of London. Service lives in Indiana with her husband and daughter.

Plot Summary

Since birth, fourteen-year-olds Connie Hendricks and Prince Rudolph periodically lose consciousness and enter each other's minds. Their respective sets of parents think they are ill, but Connie and Rudolph are determined to hide their secret friendship and protect their "visits." When Rudolph, the heir apparent, is kidnapped in a move against the monarchy, Connie realizes she must reveal their secret to help save him.

Introducing the Book

The first chapter focuses on Connie; the second chapter on Rudolph. To introduce these two main characters, read aloud to "What had they learned?" (P. 21, third paragraph, hardback edition). Consider having a male and a female reader for each part. Reading to this point will tie the characters and plot together. Because the novel features male and female protagonists, both boys and girls will enjoy reading it. Use the terrific cover art (hardback edition) to visually focus students on the main theme of this book.

Booktalks

In the Aisle

What would happen if your mind sometimes merged with someone else's? Could you keep it a secret? And what if that someone were kidnapped? What would you do then? *Being of Two Minds* has some fantastic answers.

With the Author's Words

Fourteen-year-old Connie is seeing a doctor again. It's a common occurrence. Her parents want to find out why she frequently passes out.

> *The problem was the fear—the fear that this time a doctor might find out what was wrong—and cure her. She didn't want to be cured. She had lived with this all her life. It was part of what made her her.* (P. 1, hardback edition)

What Connie lives with is the unusual ability to pass into another person's mind. That person is Rudolph, and they have enjoyed this strange communication since birth. If the doctors discover and cure this abnormality, will they each be of one mind? *Being of Two Minds* is definitely interesting!

Literature Extensions/Alternative Book Report Activities

Architecture/Castles—Rudolph is held captive in a historic castle complete with gargoyles, grottoes, turrets, and so on. Students can do further research on castles, build a model, or draw a castle floor plan. For information consult David Macaulay's *Castle* (Houghton Mifflin, 1977), Gian Paolo Ceserani and Piero Ventura's *Grand Constructions* (Putnam, 1983), Sheila Sancha's *The Castle Story* (HarperCollins, 1982), and Beth Smith's *Castles* (Franklin Watts, 1988).

Art—As Connie searches for Rudy throughout the castle, she notices a small tapestry, which she uses to help rescue Rudy. Tapestries were often used for wall coverings in the medieval period. Provide art history books that include illustrations or photographs of tapestries such as the famous Unicorn tapestry.
 Invite a weaver from your community who creates modern wall hangings or tapestry to demonstrate or present information to your class or both. Interested students can begin their own weaving projects.

Government—Rudolph is the crown prince in the fictitious country of Thulgaria. Students can study various forms of monarchy that exist in real countries throughout the world. Examine the issue of neutrality, as well. Which countries claim this as policy, and why? Consult Denis J. Fodor's *The Neutrals* (Time Life, 1982) and Gene Gurney's *Kingdoms of Europe: An Illustrated Encyclopedia of Ruling Monarchs from Ancient Times to the Present* (Crown, 1982).

Health—Connie and Rudolph have seizures similar to those suffered by epileptics. In their attempts to identify their children's conditions, their parents take them to doctors who map their brain waves using electroencephalograms (EEGs), magnetic resonance imaging (MRIs), and computerized axial tomography (CAT scans). Invite a radiologist or neurologist to explain these various technologies which are used to study abnormalities of the brain.

Pamela F. Service Wrote:

All's Faire

Being of Two Minds

A Question of Destiny

The Reluctant God

Stinker From Space

Stinker's Return

Tomorrow's Magic

Under Alien Stars

Vision Quest

Weirdos of the Universe, Unite!

When the Night Wind Howls

Winter of Magic's Return

Wizard of Wind & Rock

Your Majesty!

Alexander, Lloyd. The Westmark Trilogy

Fleischman, Sid. The Whipping Boy

Hendry, Frances Mary. Quest for a Kelpie

———. Quest for Maid

Konigsburg, E. L. A Proud Taste for Scarlet and Miniver

Pope, Elizabeth Marie. The Perilous Gard

Service, Pamela F. Being of Two Minds

Wismer, Donald. Starluck

ESP

Aaron, Chester. Out of Sight, Out of Mind

Belden, Wilanne S. Mind-Hold

DeClements, Barthe. Double Trouble

Duncan, Lois. A Gift of Magic

Gloss, Molly. Outside the Gates

Lunn, Janet. Shadow in Hawthorn Bay

Roberts, Willo Davis. The Girl with the Silver Eyes

Service, Pamela F. Being of Two Minds

Shreve, Susan
The Gift of the Girl Who Couldn't Hear

LC 91-2247, ©1991, 79p., $12.95 (ISBN 0-688-10318-9), Tambourine Books

Genre: Contemporary realistic fiction

Themes: Friendship, self-esteem, self-acceptance, theater-musicals, courage, determination, deafness, adjustment to handicaps, cliques, school life, peer relationships, cruelty

Reading level: Fourth grade

Interest level: Fifth through seventh grades

Reviews:
Booklist. 88(4):437 October 15, 1991. (Starred)
Bulletin of the Center for Children's Books.
    45(2):49 October, 1991. (Recommended)
School Library Journal. 37(8):169 August,
    1991. (Starred)

Author Information
Susan Richards Shreve was born in Toledo, Ohio, and lives in Washington, D.C., with her husband. Having written more than ten books for children and young adults, Shreve is also well-known for her adult novels. As an essayist, she makes frequent appearances on public television's "MacNeil-Lehrer News Hour." Shreve grew up with a crime reporter father who told stories and created high drama out of ordinary incidents. She began penning as a teenager, writing an autobiographical book when she was eighteen. Shreve writes, "It was quite boring and, not surprisingly, did not sell." She went to college and graduate school and didn't write again until she was thirty. Shreve says she writes the types of books she liked to read when she was a child. These are tales with rebellious heroes ("because that's the sort of child I was") and stories centered on family life. Shreve has four children, teaches at George Mason University, is a visiting professor at Columbia University, and writes for two hours each day.

Plot Summary
When Eliza turns thirteen, she also turns unsure of herself and refuses to try out for the yearly school musical, despite her long-held dream of appearing in it. Best friend Lucy is determined to try out for a part, even though she has been deaf from birth. Eliza suffers from the cruel remarks her classmates make about Lucy and her attempts to sing. Through coaching her friend, Eliza realizes Lucy's special gift is stretching beyond what most people perceive as limits.

Introducing the Book
This book is so brief, it almost seems to be a short story. The action takes place in October. Use booktalks below to entice readers or simply read aloud the first two paragraphs of chapter 1 to get readers involved.

Booktalks

In the Aisle
Eliza is a great singer but refuses to try out for the school musical. Her best friend, Lucy, who is deaf, is eager for a part herself. Eliza is determined to protect Lucy from their classmates' cruel remarks, so she develops a plan.

With the Author's Words

Eliza's best friend is Lucy.

> I love Lucy but it sometimes drives me crazy that she's deaf. She doesn't know some of the things that are important. For example, she misses the changes in the seventh-grade girls which, I suppose, is the real reason for my unhappiness. My childhood is disappearing. The friends who used to be simple dependable friends like Mary and Tricia and Dolly are not simple, or dependable any longer. Only Lucy. (P. 37, hardback edition)

More than just a dependable friend, Lucy is a generous friend. That's why this book by Susan Shreve is called *The Gift of the Girl Who Couldn't Hear*.

Literature Extensions/Alternative Book Report Activities

Drama—Students can stage and perform their own musical. Two short musicals especially suitable for performance in middle schools are Charles Schulz's *You're a Good Man, Charlie Brown* and Maurice Sendak's *Really Rosie*. The latter is based on characters from the four books in the Nutshell Library (Harper Collins Children's Books, 1962) and *The Sign on Rosie's Door* (HarperCollins Children's Books, 1960). This twenty-six minute animated video, with musical score by Carole King, is available from Weston Woods, telephone 800-243-5020. For the complete script of the Charlie Brown play, consult *You're a Good Man, Charlie Brown* with music and lyrics by Clark Gesner (Random House, 1967).

Government—As citizens we are becoming more aware of meeting the special needs of physically handicapped people. Students can research the changes occurring in federal and state regulations to eliminate physical barriers. Students interested in working with people who are physically challenged can consider volunteering for the Special Olympics, an organization that welcomes volunteers. Contact Special Olympics International, 1350 New York Avenue, NW, Suite 500, Washington, D.C. 20005, for information.

Speech/Communication—Lucy has learned to communicate by speaking and lip reading. However, many deaf individuals learn to communicate by using American Sign Language, an established alphabet of visual language.

Students can learn this alphabet with the help of Laura Rankin's picture book *The Handmade Alphabet* (Dial Books for Young Readers, 1991) and *Sign Language Talk* by Laura Greene and Eva Barash Dicken (Franklin Watts, 1989). Consider inviting a signing expert to demonstrate and teach the alphabet, phrases, and simple sentences.

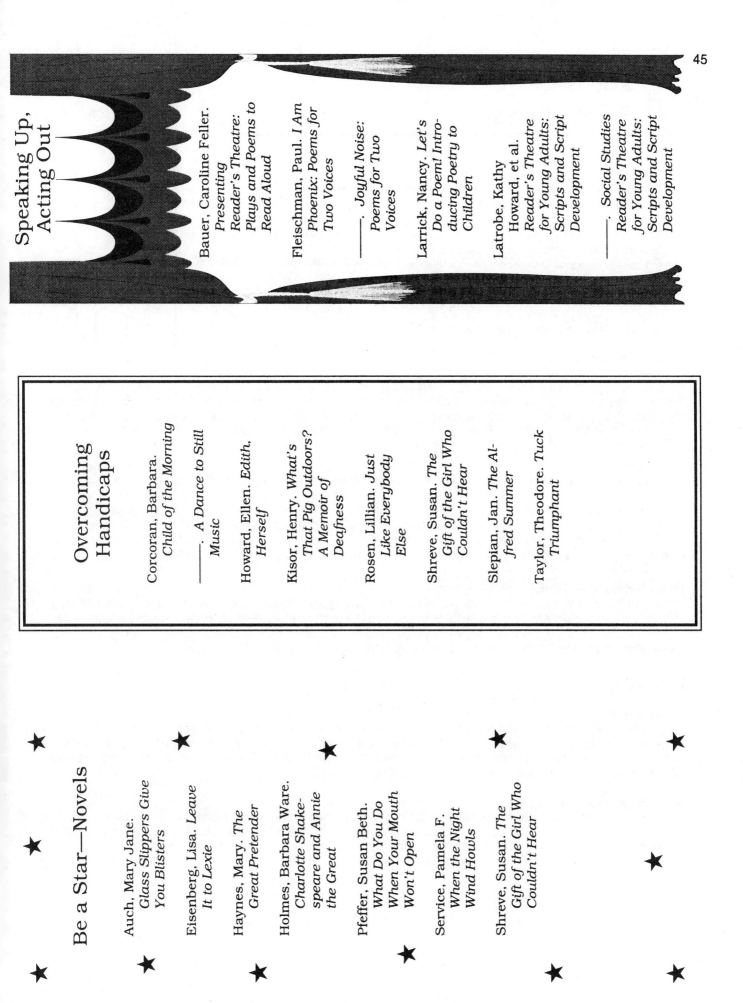

Speaking Up, Acting Out

Bauer, Caroline Feller. *Presenting Reader's Theatre: Plays and Poems to Read Aloud*

Fleischman, Paul. *I Am Phoenix: Poems for Two Voices*

———. *Joyful Noise: Poems for Two Voices*

Larrick, Nancy. *Let's Do a Poem! Introducing Poetry to Children*

Latrobe, Kathy Howard, et al. *Reader's Theatre for Young Adults: Scripts and Script Development*

———. *Social Studies Reader's Theatre for Young Adults: Scripts and Script Development*

Overcoming Handicaps

Corcoran, Barbara. *Child of the Morning*

———. *A Dance to Still Music*

Howard, Ellen. *Edith, Herself*

Kisor, Henry. *What's That Pig Outdoors? A Memoir of Deafness*

Rosen, Lillian. *Just Like Everybody Else*

Shreve, Susan. *The Gift of the Girl Who Couldn't Hear*

Slepian, Jan. *The Alfred Summer*

Taylor, Theodore. *Tuck Triumphant*

Be a Star—Novels

Auch, Mary Jane. *Glass Slippers Give You Blisters*

Eisenberg, Lisa. *Leave It to Lexie*

Haynes, Mary. *The Great Pretender*

Holmes, Barbara Ware. *Charlotte Shakespeare and Annie the Great*

Pfeffer, Susan Beth. *What Do You Do When Your Mouth Won't Open*

Service, Pamela F. *When the Night Wind Howls*

Shreve, Susan. *The Gift of the Girl Who Couldn't Hear*

Soto, Gary
Taking Sides

LC 91-11082, ©1991. 135p., $15.95 (ISBN 0-15-284076), Harcourt Brace Jovanovich

Genres: Contemporary realistic fiction, sports, multicultural

Themes: Friendship, moving, loyalty, basketball, Hispanic Americans, single-parent families, school life, cultural differences, barrio life, racism

Reading level: Fifth grade

Interest level: Sixth through ninth grades

Reviews:
Booklist. 88(7):690 December 1, 1991
Bulletin of the Center for Children's Books.
 45(3):75-76 November, 1991.
 (Recommended)
School Library Journal. 37(11):124 November, 1991
Voice of Youth Advocates. 14(5):318 December, 1991. (#3 quality, #2 popularity)

Author Information

Gary Soto is an author and a poet who grew up in California and worked as a migrant laborer as a child. He has written numerous books for adults as well as children, often using ethnicity in America as a theme. Soto's works comment on society, particularly racial tensions and poverty. His autobiographical *Living Up the Street: Narrative Recollections* (Strawberry Hill Press, 1985) won an American Book Award. Soto is a professor at the University of California, teaching English and Chicano Studies.

Plot Summary

Star basketball player Linc Mendoza has recently moved from the barrio to an affluent suburb of San Francisco. His best friend and basketball buddy, Tony, still lives in the barrio, and neither of them is looking forward to the conference basketball game between their two junior high schools. Linc still feels loyalty toward his old Hispanic neighborhood and friends and is struggling to adjust to his new school, classmates, and coach. As the game approaches, Linc faces intense internal conflicts, which he resolves during the game. Linc's story continues in the sequel *Pacific Crossing* (Harcourt Brace Jovanovich, 1992).

Introducing the Book

If you plan to read some of this aloud, the Spanish words and phrases sprinkled throughout the text may require pronunciation practice. Invite a Spanish speaking student to help, and refer to the glossary for definitions. Read aloud the first chapter to show readers how to understand the Spanish: through context clues, immediate translation within the text, or by referring to the glossary.

Booktalks

In the Aisle

When your old school plays your new school in basketball, whom do you cheer for? If you're the best player on the team, what do you do? This happens to Linc when he moves from the inner city to the suburbs, leaving old friends and teammates behind. His new coach is hard to deal with—he doesn't seem to like Hispanic kids. And Linc—he's the star of both teams.

With the Author's Words

Linc's mother was determined to leave the barrio after their home was burglarized. But their new life in an upper-class neighborhood does not necessarily mean total safety. Linc is taking a nap when he wakes up to discover a burglary in process. When he tries to stop the burglar, the man runs away.

The intruder didn't look back. He was out the door and down the porch steps before Lincoln could stop him. "Don't come back!" Lincoln screamed, fists curled tightly. "I'll mess with you, man." (P. 95, hardback edition)

Life in the 'burbs may not be as great as Linc's mom had hoped. But Linc has even more to cope with in Gary Soto's *Taking Sides.*

Literature Extensions/Alternative Book Report Activities

Home Economics—Linc's mother prepares Mexican food as part of her busy daily routine. Some of the foods mentioned are huevos rancheros, chili verde, enchiladas, and tortillas. Students can prepare and share some of these dishes. Numerous Mexican cookbooks are available in public and school library collections.

Language Arts/Poetry—Soto is recognized as a fine poet who writes from his childhood experiences. Provide some of his books of poetry for reading and discussion. Some students may be inspired to write similar verses about their own lives or neighborhoods. Provide *The Poet's Pen: Writing Poetry with Middle and High School Students* by Betty Bonham Lies (Libraries Unlimited, 1993) for specific suggestions and practical advice on teaching poetry writing.

Neighborhood Odes (Harcourt Brace Jovanovich, 1992) and *A Fire in My Hands* (Scholastic, 1991) are two recent Soto collections.

Social Studies/Business—Linc's mother is a graphic artist who started her own business. She works long and hard hours and has become very successful. Many communities provide assistance for entrepreneurs through small business incubator projects and special library book collections. The federal government offers assistance through the Small Business Administration. What services are available in your community? Students can develop their own prototype businesses, filling out the required forms, interviewing the appropriate officials, and so on.

Social Studies/Cultural Awareness—Students can use Soto's book as a springboard for exploring cultural differences, similarities, and traditions within their classroom or community. Possible activities could include interviewing adults representing various cultures, researching and discussing the community's demographic statistics, and sharing a cultural tradition or food.

Spanish/Foreign Language—The frequent use of Spanish words and phrases throughout the text in this novel can be an introduction to learning Spanish. If Spanish or other languages are not taught in your school, consider introducing your students to foreign languages via instructional tapes or classroom visitors fluent in other languages.

Provide bilingual books such as *Family Pictures/Cuardos de Familia* by Carmen Lomas Garza (Children's Book Press, 1990) and *Diego* by Jonah Winter (Alfred A. Knopf, 1991). The Diego picture book focuses on the life of the famous Mexican artist Diego Rivera with a look at his art as well as the Mexican culture. Consult *Booklist* 87(3):347-48, October 1, 1990, for the annotated bibliography of "Bilingual Books in Spanish and English for Children" for other recommended titles.

Shooting Hoops

Brooks, Bruce. *The Moves Make the Man*

Campbell, Nelson, ed. *Grass Roots & Schoolyards: A High School Basketball Anthology*

Christopher, Matt. *Red-Hot Hightops*

Dygard, Thomas. *Rebound Caper*

Halercrift, David. *Benched!*

Hallowell, Tommy. *Jester in the Backcourt*

Hughes, Dean. *Nutty Can't Miss*

Myers, Walter Dean. *Hoops*

———. *Mouse Rap*

Soto, Gary. *Taking Sides*

Tunis, John R. *Go, Team, Go!*

Hispanic Authors

Ada, Alma Flor. *Gold Coin*

Adler, C. S. *Kiss the Clown*

Argueta, Manlio. *Magic Dogs of the Volcanoes*

Bethancourt, T. Ernesto. *The Me Inside of Me*

———. *Where the Deer and the Cantaloupe Play*

Buchanan, William. *One Last Time*

Cervantes, Esther D. *Barrio Ghosts*

Garcia, Richard. *My Aunt Otilia's Spirits*

Hernandez, Irene B. *Across the Great River*

Mohr, Nicholasa. *Going Home*

City Life

Brooks, Bruce. *The Moves Make the Man*

Holman, Felice. *Slake's Limbo*

Murphy, Barbara. *Ace Hits Rock Bottom*

———. *Ace Hits the Big Time*

Myers, Walter Dean. *Mouse Rap*

———. *Scorpions*

Soto, Gary. *Taking Sides*

Strasser, Todd. *Angel Dust Blues*

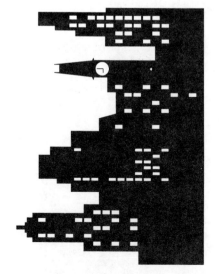

Spinelli, Jerry
There's a Girl in My Hammerlock

LC 91-8765. ©1991, 199p., $13.00 (ISBN 0-671-74684-7), Simon & Schuster

Genres: Contemporary realistic fiction, sports, humor

Themes: Gender roles, sexism, wrestling, family life, school life, peer relationships, boy-girl relationships, competition, self-esteem, perseverance, skill development, courage

Reading level: Fourth grade

Reviews:
Booklist. 88(4):441 October 15, 1991
Bulletin of the Center for Children's Books.
    45(1):23 September, 1991. (Recommended)
School Library Journal. 37(9):260 September,
    1991. (Starred)
Voice of Youth Advocates. 14(5):318 December, 1991. (#4 quality, #4 popularity)

Author Information

Jerry Spinelli was born in Norristown, Pennsylvania. He and his wife, Eileen, also a writer, have six children. One of his first writing experiences was writing a poem after his high school football team won a big game. It was published in the local newspaper, and Spinelli has been writing ever since. His first book, *Space Station Seventh Grade*, was not intended as a young adult novel, however, the story of the protagonist's thirteenth year accidentally pushed Spinelli into the young adult field. He is interested in writing for children of various ages. Spinelli's personal philosophy is that we learn far more from our failures than we do from our successes (and we experience infinitely more failures!). He feels that students need training in how to accept and build on failure.

Plot Summary

Thirteen-year-old Maisie decides to join the wrestling team after failing to make the cheerleading squad. Initially her reason is to get close to Eric DeLong, her first crush. But ultimately it becomes a challenge to make the team and be accepted as a teammate despite her sex. Though the coach is less than encouraging at the start, he becomes one of her greatest champions. The physical and mental trials and tribulations of competing in a traditionally male sport, as well as dealing with the adverse publicity and negative peer comments, are as challenging as learning the sport itself.

Introducing the Book

Even though the reading level is relatively low, the length of this novel may put off reluctant readers. Help them become enthralled in this fast-paced novel by reading aloud the first five or six chapters (27 to 33 pages). The action begins in September, so that's an appropriate time to introduce this book, which appeared on ALA/YALSA's Recommended Books for the Reluctant Young Adult Reader list in 1992.

Booktalks

In the Aisle

Some people don't think girls should compete with boys in sports. Other people think girls should have a chance, if they're good enough. Maisie hopes she's good enough to wrestle on her junior high school team. But some people don't think that's a good idea. What do you think?

With the Author's Words

Against everyone's advice, Maisie Potter is trying to make the junior high wrestling team. Her teammates seem disgusted with her, her friends won't talk to her, and even the coach doesn't seem to like her. On the last day of practice before the final team is selected, Maisie doesn't think she has a chance.

> The coach was in my face. "Escape, Potter! Escape!" I went wild. I pushed, shoved, wrenched, kicked. I did everything but spit, and suddenly—I was out. Standing face-to-face with Eric DeLong. The whistle blew. "Okay, first group, laps! Second group onto the mats! Let's go, people! Move!" I went out with the first group. I ran the hallways in a daze. I made the team! I couldn't believe it. (Pp. 73-74, hardback edition)

Maisie may wish she hadn't. She's the "girl in my hammerlock" in Jerry Spinelli's funny and exciting book.

Literature Extensions/Alternative Book Report Activities

Creative Writing—Students can put themselves in Maisie's place when her mother appears one night to be "best friends." How would they respond to such a visit from a mother or a father?

Government/Physical Education—Title IX, a federal law enacted in 1972, requires schools and institutions to provide equal sports opportunities for men and women. Students can expand their understanding of this law by researching the history of its development or specific cases of boys or girls participating in sports previously restricted by gender. Start by looking at "The Slow Track" by Alexander Wolff, in *Sports Illustrated* 77(13):52+, September 28, 1992, for a look at elusive equity for women in high school and college sports.

Language Arts—Spinelli begins and ends *There's a Girl in My Hammerlock* with parts from a long letter Maisie writes to the editor of the local newspaper. Keeping in mind that most newspapers limit the length of letters, encourage students to select a topic that they are interested in and write their opinions. Sending these on to the paper is left to the discretion of each student.

Physical Education/Wrestling—Invite a wrestler or coach to demonstrate takedowns, escapes, control moves, pinning holds, and so on, to your class. Provide books such as Ron Fox's *Wrestling Basics* (Prentice, 1986) and Tom Jarman and Reid Hanley's *Wrestling for Beginners* (Contemporary Books, 1983) for students who wish to learn more about the sport. *Rules of the Game* by the Diagram Group (St. Martins Press, 1990) is an illustrated encyclopedia of more than 150 sports.

Social Issues/Chauvinism—Gender equity is a strong theme in Spinelli's novel. Maisie's parents are supportive of the choices she makes regardless of the chauvinistic opinions of others. Discuss this issue and provide Anthony Browne's *Piggybook* (Alfred A. Knopf, 1986), "a wickedly feminist tale." This picture book for all ages is for anybody with a sense of humor and a desire for social justice. Use *Piggybook* as a springboard for discussions regarding family responsibilities and roles. Examine the illustrations carefully for hidden details.

Jerry Spinelli Wrote:

Dump Days

Jason and Marceline

Maniac Magee

Night of the Whale

Space Station Seventh Grade

There's a Girl in My Hammerlock

Who Put That Hair in My Toothbrush?

Takedown—Wrestling Stories

Christopher, Matt. *Takedown*

Crutcher, Chris. *Athletic Shorts*

Dacquino, V. T. *Kiss the Candy Days Good-Bye*

Gutman, Bill. *Strange & Amazing Wrestling Stories*

Killien, Christi. *Rusty Ferlanger, Lady's Man*

Klass, David. *Wrestling with Honor*

Salassi, Otto R. *On the Ropes*

Spinelli, Jerry. *There's a Girl in My Hammerlock*

Girls in Boys' Sports

Cebulash, Mel. The Ruth Marini series

Crutcher, Chris. *Athletic Shorts*

Dygard, Thomas J. *Forward Pass*

Emerson, Mark. *The Mean Lean Weight-lifting Queen*

Gregorich, Barbara. *She's on First*

Kaplan, Janice. *First Ride*

Klass, David. *A Different Season*

Knudson, R. A. *Zanbanger*

Korman, Gordon. *The Zucchini Warriors*

Spinelli, Jerry. *There's a Girl in My Hammerlock*

Tolkien, J. R. R.
The Hobbit; or, There and Back Again

LC 89-92604, ©1989, unpaged, $12.95 (ISBN 0-345-36858-4), First Eclipse/Ballantine Books

Illustrated by David Wenzel. Adapted by Charles Dixon with Sean Deming.

Genres: Graphic novel (comic book or trade comic), fantasy, adventure

Themes: Good versus evil, the heroic quest, cleverness, courage, loyalty, luck, greed, war, wizards, dwarves, dragons, goblins, giants, treasure

Reading level: Sixth grade

Interest level: Fifth through twelfth grades

Reviews:
Booklist. 88(1):45 September 1, 1991

Author Information

To many readers J. R. R. Tolkien (1892-1973) still lives. His epic fantasy trilogy, *The Lord of the Rings*, transcends time and is continually read throughout the world. Born in South Africa to British parents, Tolkien ultimately grew up in England. He was a professor at Pembroke College, Oxford, from 1925 to 1945, and then served as Merton Professor of English Language and Literature until his retirement in 1959. A language expert, Tolkien was fascinated by the linguistic and literary traditions of the English West Midlands, but his long-lasting fame is due to his detailed creation of Middle-earth. See "Literature Extensions" on page 53 for a list of Tolkien biographies.

Plot summary

This abridged and illustrated version of Tolkien's fantasy novel *The Hobbit* chronicles the adventures of thirteen dwarves and Bilbo Baggins as they set off to reclaim a treasure guarded by Smaug, the dragon. With luck and cunning, the adventurers survive encounters with goblins, giants, wolves, spiders, and other creatures of Middle-earth. Bilbo's tenacity and magic ring, as well as the wizard Gandalf's assistance, help make their quest a success.

Introducing the Book

When potential readers are aware of the graphic novel (comic book) format of this fantasy, they'll need no further selling. Use it to introduce the unabridged version of Tolkien's *The Hobbit* as well as the entire Lord of the Rings trilogy. Consult Katharyn F. Crabbe's *J. R. R. Tolkien* (Frederick Ungar, 1981) for biographical information and specifics concerning *The Hobbit* and the Lord of the Rings trilogy. Provide the revised edition of *The Atlas of Middle Earth* by Kevin Wynn Fonstad (Houghton Mifflin, 1992) for "geographic" information.

Booktalks

In the Aisle

Hobbits never were big on having adventures or having unexpected things happen to them. Bilbo Baggins was no exception! At least he wasn't until Gandalf, the wizard, convinced Bilbo to accompany thirteen dwarves on their quest to recover their treasure. Then something "Tookish" came over Bilbo, and the rest is history and his-story.

With the Author's Words

The wizard Gandalf is sending Bilbo Baggins and thirteen dwarves through Mirkwood Forest with a warning to not leave the track. He wishes them luck, for he knows they'll need it to make it safely through to the other side.

> *It was as dark in the forest in the morning as at night, and very secret: "a sort of watching and waiting feeling," Bilbo said to himself. There were black squirrels in the wood and Bilbo caught glimpses of them scuttling behind tree trunks. There were queer noises too, grunts, scufflings, and hurryings in the undergrowth; but what made the noises even Bilbo's sharp inquisitive eyes could not see.* (P. 70)

Bilbo and his group have already had altercations with elves, goblins, a giant bear, and a creepy Middle-earth creature named Gollum. What could be lurking in Mirkwood Forest? You will *see* and read all about it when you experience this illustrated version of *The Hobbit.*

Literature Extensions/Alternative Book Report Activities

Art—This version of *The Hobbit* has appealing artwork that moves the story along, accurately capturing events and characters. Artist David Wenzel says his artwork was inspired by that of artists Arthur Rackham, Howard Pyle, and Hal Foster.

Provide students with examples of these artists' work as well as Will Eisner's *Comics & Sequential Art* (Poorhouse Press, 1990). For budding comic book artists, obtain the video *The Masters of Comic Book Art* (Ken Viola Productions, 1987), which includes interviews with ten of the great comic book artists along with examples of their work.

Games—Enlarge the Wilderland map located in the frontispiece of *The Hobbit.* Students can develop and design a board game to include goblins, trolls, wizards, dragons, elves, Gollum, spiders, Wargs, dwarves, eagles, Lake-men, the magic ring, hobbits, and other elements of fantasy. Ray J. Marran's *Table Games: How to Make and How to Play Them* (A.S. Barnes, 1976) can be used as a reference.

Geography/Maps/Orienteering—Reading *The Hobbit* is enhanced by the use of the colorful map included in this illustrated volume. Students can study further about maps and map making by referring to *The New Explorer's Guide to Using Maps and Compasses* by Percy W. Blandford (TAB Books, 1992), *The Sierra Club Wayfinding Book* by Vicki McVey (Sierra Club Books, 1989), *Maps: Getting from Here to There* by Harvey Weiss (Houghton Mifflin, 1991), and *How Maps Are Made* by John Baynes (Facts on File, 1987).

Crossing through unknown lands as Bilbo and the dwarves did is somewhat like orienteering. Orienteering is a sport that traditionally uses a topographical map and a compass. Participants navigate their way between checkpoints along an unfamiliar course somewhat similar to a scavenger hunt. Contact your public library to see if an orienteering club exists in your region. Find out if someone would be willing to speak to your class about such events. If possible, take your students orienteering.

Literature—Develop a classroom library for Tolkien fans to "read all about it." Related materials would include the complete Lord of the Rings trilogy; other versions of *The Hobbit,* such as the volume illustrated by Michael Hague (Houghton Mifflin, 1984); Tolkien's *The Silmarillion* edited by Christopher Tolkien (Houghton Mifflin, 1977); Tolkien's *The Tolkien Reader* (Ballantine Books, 1966); *A Tolkien Bestiary* by David Day (Ballantine Books, 1979); and *The Tolkien Scrapbook* edited by Alida Becker (Running Press, 1978). Biographies of Tolkien include *J.R.R. Tolkien: Master of Fantasy* by David R. Collins (Lerner, 1992), *The Biography of J.R.R. Tolkien: Architect of Middle-earth* by Daniel Grotta (Running Press, 1978), *J.R.R. Tolkien* by Deborah Webster Rogers and Ivor A. Rogers (Macmillan, 1980), *Tolkien: The Illustrated Encyclopedia* by David Day (Collier, 1991), and *The Authorized Biography of Tolkien* by Humphrey Carpenter (Houghton Mifflin, 1977).

A tribute to Tolkien celebrating the 100th anniversary of his birth is available in *After the King: Stories in Honor of J.R.R. Tolkien* edited by Martin H. Greenberg (Tor Books, 1992). Here nineteen authors write new stories of Middle-earth.

Audio versions of Tolkien's books are available from Mind's Eye Audiotapes; an animated video version of *The Hobbit* (1983) is offered by ABC Video Enterprises.

Dragon Tales

Baskin, Hosie, and Leonard Baskin. *A Book of Dragons*

Bradshaw, Gillian. *The Dragon and the Thief*

Dickinson, Peter. *The Flight of Dragons*

Fletcher, Susan. *Dragon's Milk*

McCaffrey, Anne. *Dragonsong*

McKinley, Robin. *The Hero and the Crown*

Sargent, Sarah. *Weird Henry Berg*

Velde, Vivian Vande. *Dragon's Bait*

Wrede, Patricia. *Dealing with Dragons*

——. *Searching for Dragons*

Yep, Laurence. *Dragons of the Lost Sea*

Yolen, Jane. *The Pit Dragon series*

Places Like Middle-Earth

Alexander, Lloyd. *The Chronicles of Prydain*

Brooks, Terry. *The Shannara series*

Card, Orson Scott. *The Tales of Alvin Maker series*

Chetwin, Grace. *The Tales of Gom series*

Christopher, John. *The Winchester Trilogy*

Harris, Geraldine. *The Seven Citadels quartet*

Jacques, Brian. *The Redwall series*

LeGuin, Ursula. *The Earthsea Trilogy*

McKillip, Patricia A. *The Star-Bearer Trilogy*

Pierce, Tamora. *The Alanna series*

Weis, Margaret. *The Dragonlance books*

Graphic Novel—A longer and more sophisticated version of comic books.

These self-contained stories use text and artwork to advance the plot and set new visual standards. These longer short stories or short novels are usually the size of a magazine.

Eisner, Will. *The Dreamer*

Gibson, Henry, and Alfredo P. Alcala. *The Gift: The Illustrated History of the Statue of Liberty*

Mason, Patrick. *Wolfgang Amadeus Mozart's The Magic Flute*

Pini, Wendy. *Beauty and the Beast: Night of Beauty*

——. *Beauty and the Beast: Portrait of Love*

Pini, Wendy and Richard Pini. *The Elfquest series*

Shanower, Eric. *The Forgotten Forest of Oz*

Tolkien, J. R. R., and David Wenzel. *The Hobbit*

Truman, Timothy. *Wilderness: The True Story of Simon Girty, the Renegade*

Zelenetz, Alan, et al. *The Raven Banner: A Tale of Asgard*

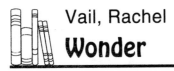

Vail, Rachel
Wonder

LC 91-10576, ©1991, 122p., $13.95 (ISBN 0-531-05964-2; ISBN 0-531-08564-3, library binding), Orchard Books

Genres: Contemporary realistic fiction, humor

Themes: Friendship, junior high school, peer relationships, cliques, boy-girl relationships, self-esteem, ridicule, family problems, loneliness

Reading level: Fourth grade

Interest level: Fifth through eighth grades

Reviews:
Booklist. 88(1):54 September 1, 1991
Bulletin of the Center for Children's Books. 45(1):24 September, 1991. (Recommended and starred)
School Library Journal. 37(8):196 August, 1991. (Starred)
Voice of Youth Advocates. 14(4):234 October, 1991. (#3 quality, #4 popularity)

Author Information
Wonder is Rachel Vail's first novel. After graduating from Georgetown University in Washington, D.C., Vail returned home to New Rochelle, New York. She remembers everything about her seventh-grade year.

Plot Summary
Jessica's first-person account of starting seventh grade is finely balanced between the agony and the humor of early adolescence. When her best friend deserts her for a new group of friends, Jessica is plunged into loneliness and insecurity. Having a first boyfriend doesn't make it any easier, despite his patience and loyalty.

Introducing the Book
Attention adults: Read this book yourselves. If you live with, work with, or substitute teach early adolescents, this novel is a must. To introduce it to students, merely read the first sentence ("Junior high sucks!") or the first chapter. They'll take it from there. Because the action takes place at the beginning of the school year, it is appropriate to read it at that time. The flip-side companion to *Wonder* is Vail's *Do-Over* (Orchard Books, 1992).

Booktalks

In the Aisle
When Jessica starts seventh grade, life is terrible for her. She has been abandoned by her best friend, eats lunch alone, and is being teased about her new dress for school. Do you think she survives? I *Wonder*, too.

With the Author's Words

> *I sat alone at lunch again today. Everybody's worst nightmare. I pretended I was so into reading my book that I didn't want to be bothered even unwrapping my tuna sandwich, not that I read word one.... The insides of my cheeks are all messed up from where I was chomping down, but no way was I giving anyone the satisfaction of seeing me cry.* (P. 13, hardback edition)

Starting junior high is hard enough, but when Jessica is deserted by her best friend, things seem as though they will never be right again. Do you *Wonder* what will happen?

Literature Extensions/Alternative Book Report Activities

Art—Many schools provide opportunities for students to play games, have contests, and socialize during lunch or after school. Consider instituting a similar program at your school if one doesn't exist. One activity might be to collect and borrow Etch-A-Sketch boards for student use. As Jessica and her brother did, students can create on the boards. Their final products could be displayed or judged.

Art/Home Economics—Like the kids in Jessica's class who attend a Halloween party, your students can create costumes. You may wish to select categories such as literary characters (the Princess and the Pea, Dorothy in Oz), product advertising (Wonderbread, California Raisins, the Fruit of the Loom guys), inventions (a computer, robot), and so on. See the Bookmark on page 57 for books on making costumes.

Life Skills/Sociology—Every school has cliques, and many students feel they do not fit in. Discuss coping skills and provide books for further information. Some helpful titles are *Growing & Changing: A Handbook for Preteens* by Kathy McCoy and Charles Wibbelsman (Putnam, 1987), *Get Help Solving the Problems in Your Life* by Sara Gilbert (Morrow Junior Books, 1989), and *How to Survive as a Teen: When No One Understands* by Stevan E. Atanasoff (Herald Press, 1989). For further fictional reading, provide William Goldman's *Lord of the Flies* (Coward-McCann, 1978), because it fits into this curriculum area and is mentioned in *Wonder*.

Mathematics—Jessica's father's business is on the verge of bankruptcy due to dishonest accounting by his partner. Invite an accountant to your class to discuss his or her job and to show examples of spreadsheets, ledgers, and so on.

Jessica learns about the stock market from her grandmother, who is interested in the Crayola Company. Another math tie-in would be to have students select a stock that interests them and chart its activity over a period of several months. Provide the daily *Wall Street Journal* so students can learn to read stock tables.

Books for Making Costumes

Asher, Jane. *Jane Asher's Fancy Dress*

Cummings, Richard. *101 Costumes for All Ages, All Occasions*

Greenhowe, Jean. *Costumes for Nursery Tale Characters*

Rowland-Warner, L. *Costume*

Walker, Mark. *Creative Costumes for Any Occasion*

If you loved *Wonder* by Rachel Vail, you'll like:

♂

Byars, Betsy. *Bingo Brown and the Meaning of Love*

Gilson, Jamie. *Hobie Hanson, Greatest Hero of the Mall*

Greer, Gery, and Bob Ruddick. *This Island Isn't Big Enough for the Four of Us!*

Kiesel, Stanley. *The War Between the Pitiful Teachers and the Splendid Kids*

Korman, Gordon. *The Twinkie Squad*

Lord, Athena. *Z.A.P., Zoe, and the Musketeers*

Lowry, Lois. *Your Move, J. P.*

Spinelli, Jerry. *Space Station Seventh Grade*

Wardlaw, Lee. *Seventh-Grade Weirdo*

If you loved *Wonder* by Rachel Vail, you'll like:

♀

Auch, Mary Jane. *Glass Slippers Give You Blisters*

Blume, Judy. *Just as Long as We're Together*

Keller, Beverly. *Desdemona—Twelve Going on Desperate*

Lowry, Lois. *Anastasia on Her Own*

Naylor, Phyllis Reynolds. *All but Alice*

Okimoto, Jean Davies. *Take a Chance, Gramps!*

Woodson, Jacqueline
The Dear One

LC 90-46677, ©1991, 145p., $14.00 (ISBN 0-385-30416-1), Delacorte Press

Genre: Contemporary realistic fiction, multicultural

Themes: Teen pregnancy, friendship, black communities, self-esteem, single-parent families, mothers and daughters, intergenerational relationships, death, interracial class conflicts, lesbianism, jealousy, adoption, loyalty, alcoholism, divorce

Reading level: Fifth grade

Interest level: Fifth through tenth grade

Reviews:
Bulletin of the Center for Children's Books.
    45(1):26 September, 1991. (Recommended)
Horn Book. 67(6):746 November/December, 1991
School Library Journal. 37(6):129 June, 1991
Voice of Youth Advocates. 14(4):236 October, 1991. (#4 quality, #4 popularity)

Author Information
Born in Ohio, Jacqueline Woodson grew up in South Carolina and lives in Brooklyn, New York. Woodson is a drama therapist in addition to being a writer. She also works with homeless children and runaways in New York City shelters.

Plot Summary
Twelve-year-old Feni has a comfortable life with her mother, Catherine, in a wealthy black Pennsylvania suburb. To Feni's dismay, fifteen-year-old Rebecca comes from Harlem to spend her last trimester of pregnancy with them. Initially, Feni resents Rebecca. However, the strong female network established by Catherine and her friends, Marion and Bernadette, provides a loving and caring environment in which both teens mature and flourish. At first, Rebecca considers Marion and Bernadette's lesbian relationship undesirable, but eventually she develops an understanding and appreciation for each of them.

Introducing the Book
Brimming with sensitive issues from the very first paragraph, this novel is an honest and forthright look at strong female friends and relationships. Booktalking is a better choice for selling this book than reading it aloud. *The Dear One* was included on the ALA/YALSA's Recommended Books for the Reluctant Young Adult Reader list, 1992.

Booktalks

In the Aisle
At first Feni can't stand Rebecca. Her comfortable life is rudely interrupted when Rebecca arrives to spend the last months of her pregnancy in Feni's house. But sometimes good things happen when you least expect it.

With the Author's Words
Twelve-year-old Feni remembers:

> *My grandmother once told me that all it takes is for one tiny thing to happen and then, Boom! your life is changed forever. That's what I'm trying to remember now—the one tiny thing. The thing that might have happened to Rebecca before she came, the thing that happened to me after she was here. Because by the time she left, we were different people, all of us—her, me, Mama—even Marion.* (P. 2, hardback edition)

Rebecca is fifteen and pregnant. The changes she'll face seem obvious, but how does this affect Feni, Mama, and Marion? And, who is *The Dear One*?

Literature Extensions/Alternative Book Report Activities

Health/Alcoholism—Feni's mother is a recovering alcoholic. Provide information about this devastating disease that can destroy families. Books available on this subject include *Living on the Edge: A Guide to Intervention for Families with Drug and Alcohol Problems* by Katherine Ketcham (Bantam Books, 1989), *Not My Family: The Truth About Alcoholism* by Maxine B. Rosenberg (Bradbury Press, 1988), *When Your Parent Drinks Too Much: A Book for Teenagers* by Eric Ryerson (Facts on File, 1985), and *Everything You Need to Know About an Alcoholic Parent* by Nancy Shuker (Rosen, 1989).

Health/Vegetarians—Rebecca doesn't eat meat, which poses a challenge for the cooking and eating practices of Feni's family. Eating less meat is a current health trend, and the number of vegetarians has grown in the last several decades. Eating balanced meals without meat is not as difficult as it sounds. Students can research the benefits of a vegetarian diet by referring to *The Vegetarian Teen* by Charles A. Salter (Millbrook Press, 1991) or *Going Vegetarian: A Guide for Teenagers* by Sada Fretz and Eric Fretz (Morrow, 1983).

Try experimenting with vegetarian recipes. Consult *Sundays at Moosewood Restaurant* by the Moosewood Collective (Simon & Schuster, 1990), *Glories of the Vegetarian Table: A Collection of Contemporary Vegetarian Recipes and Menus* by Janet Hazen (Aris Books, 1988), *The Gradual Vegetarian* by Lisa Tracy (M. Evans, 1985), and *The Savory Way* by Deborah Madison (Bantam Books, 1990).

For a vegetarian newsletter written by and for teenagers, contact Vegetarian Education Network, P.O. Box 3347, West Chester, PA 19381, for their publication *How On Earth!*

Social Studies/Africa—Feni is a nickname for Afenie, which means "the dear one" in Swahili. For further information about this language and culture, provide these interesting and beautifully illustrated picture books representing African cultures and language: *Rabbit Makes a Monkey Out of Lion: A Swahili Tale* by Verna Aardema (Dial Books for Young Readers, 1989), and *Ashanti to Zulu: African Traditions* by Margaret Musgrove (Dial Books for Young Readers, 1976), an unusual alphabet book representing various African cultures from an anthropological stance.

Other appropriate books include *Moja Means One: Swahili Counting Book* by Muriel Feelings (Dial Books for Young Readers, 1987), *Jambo Means Hello: Swahili Alphabet Book* by Muriel Feelings and Tom Feelings (Dial Books for Young Readers, 1985), *Count Your Way Through Africa* by James Haskins (Carolrhoda Books, 1989) and *Hyena and the Moon! Stories to Tell from Kenya* (Libraries Unlimited, 1994).

Social Studies/Family Structure—Feni's strong extended family consists of her mother and her mother's two friends. Today's changing society forces a look at redefining "family" in light of single-parent homes, couples without children, gay or lesbian households, "blended" families, adoptive parents, interracial families, and so on.

For further exploration on this issue refer students to books such as Kathlyn Gay's *Changing Families: Meeting Today's Challenges* (Enslow, 1988), *The Rainbow Effect: Interracial Families* (Franklin Watts, 1987), *The Family* by Dianne Hales (Chelsea House, 1988), and *The American Family* by Richard Worth (Franklin Watts, 1984).

Teen Novels:
The Issue Is Drinking

Barr, Linda. *The Wrong Way Out*

Fosburgh, Liza. *Cruise Control*

Fox, Paula. *The Moonlight Man*

Levy, Marilyn. *Touching*

Mazer, Harry. *The War on Villa Street*

Sandlin, Tim. *Skipped Parts*

Wersba, Barbara. *Crazy Vanilla*

Woodson, Jacqueline. *The Dear One*

Featuring Proud
Black Girls

Hamilton, Virginia. *Cousins*

———. *Sweet Whispers, Brother Rush*

Hurmence, Belinda. *Tancy*

Tate, Eleanor. *The Secret of Gumbo Grove*

Taylor, Mildred D. *The Road to Memphis*

Voigt, Cynthia. *Come a Stranger*

Walter, Mildred Pitts. *Trouble's Child*

Woodson, Jacqueline. *The Dear One*

———. *Maizon at Blue Hill*

Yarborough, Camille. *The Shimmershine Queens*

All Kinds of Families

Block, Francesca Lia. *Weetzie Bat*

Byars, Betsy. The *Blossom Family* series

Cannon, A. E. *Amazing Gracie*

Koertge, Ron. *The Arizona Kid*

Lowry, Lois. *Rabble Starkey*

Naylor, Phyllis Reynolds. The *Alice* series

Okimoto, Jean Davies. *Jason's Women*

Sachs, Marilyn. *Circles*

Smith, Doris B. *Return to Bitter Creek*

Woodson, Jacqueline. *The Dear One*

———. *Maizon at Blue Hill*

Yolen, Jane
Wizard's Hall

LC 90-45445, ©1991, 133p., $13.95 (ISBN 0-15-298132-2), Harcourt Brace Jovanovich

Genre: Fantasy

Themes: Wizards, magic, schools, homesickness, fear, self-confidence, courage, friendship, good versus evil, monsters, perseverance, destiny

Reading level: Fifth grade

Interest level: Fourth through seventh grades

Reviews:
Booklist. 87(14):1494 March 15, 1991
Bulletin of the Center for Children's Books. 44(11):280 July/August, 1991
School Library Journal. 37(7):75-76 July, 1991
Voice of Youth Advocates. 14(3):184-85 August, 1991. (#5 quality, #2 popularity)

Author Information
Prolific author Jane Yolen has written more than one hundred books for readers of all ages and is the winner of numerous awards. She grew up in New York City and developed a sense of marvel that she has never lost. When asked if she believes in magic, Yolen replied, "I believe that everything around us is touched by magic if we just look long enough and deep enough."

Plot Summary
Henry isn't sure what he wants to be, but when he casually mentions an interest in wizardry, his ma packs him off to Wizard's Hall, posthaste. Upon his arrival, Henry is renamed Thornmallow ("prickly on the outside, squishy within") and discovers his critical role in saving Wizard's Hall from the evils of the Master and the Beast.

Introducing the Book
Read aloud the prologue and chapter 1 to hook potential readers. Direct students' attention to the clear chapter headings that aptly foreshadow upcoming events.

Booktalks

In the Aisle
If you added up all the little bits of evil and badness in the world and put them into one being, it might be a terrible Beast. And that's what is threatening Wizard's Hall when Henry arrives for his apprenticeship. He's the 113th student, the one who is destined to save the school, and the world. Can he do it?

With the Author's Words
When Thornmallow arrives at Wizard's Hall to learn the art of wizardry, things have been going badly there for some time. Something evil is afoot.

> [T]he fact remains that Thornmallow meant well. And he tried. He came to Wizard's Hall at the time of its greatest peril, the 113th student, the very last to be admitted in that horrible year. And it turned out the inhabitants of Wizard's Hall were glad indeed that Thornmallow studied there. Not because he was the world's greatest wizard. But because he meant well. And he tried. (Pp. ix-x, hardback edition)

But is just trying enough? Can Wizard's Hall be saved? Jane Yolen's fast fantasy tells the story.

Literature Extensions/Alternative Book Report Activities

Careers—Henry changes his mind frequently regarding his chosen career. What do you want to be? How often have you changed your mind? Provide students with general books on careers such as Sue Alexander's *Finding Your First Job* (Dutton Children's Books, 1980) and Neil Johnson's *All in a Day's Work: Twelve Americans Talk About Their Jobs* (Little, Brown, 1989). Titles on specific careers also can be made available.

Language Arts—Henry regularly remembers his ma's words of wisdom. It seems as though she had proverbs for many occasions and situations. One was: "Hunger is a great seasoner" (P. 4, hardback edition). Students can collect the proverbs in *Wizard's Hall*, make a list of proverbs used in their own families, or write their own.

Use this as an opportunity to introduce students to quotation reference books such as *Instant Quotation Dictionary* compiled by Donald O. Bolander, et al. (Career, 1988), *The New Portable Curmudgeon* compiled and edited by Jon Winokur (New American Library, 1987), or *Bartlett's Familiar Quotations.*

Language Arts/Names—Each student at Wizard's Hall is renamed according to his character or ability. "You are like your name and it is like you. They *correspond*" (P. 93, hardback edition). Henry's new name is Thornmallow, "prickly on the outside, squishy within." Does your name suit you? What is the true meaning of your name?

To answer these questions, provide students with books on names such as Barbara Shook Hazen's *Last, First, Middle and Nick: All About Names* (Prentice-Hall, 1979), Mary Price Lee and Richard S. Lee's *Last Names First:... and Some First Names, Too* (Westminster, 1985), and Milton Meltzer's *A Book About Names* (HarperCollins Children's Books, 1984).

Science—In Henry's room, the ceiling becomes a star map and a magical voice announces the names of the constellations as they blink on and off. Use this idea as a springboard for further study of the constellations. Students can recreate Henry's ceiling and make their own announcements, build models of various constellations, or do further reading.

Suggested titles include *The Sky Observer's Guide* by Newton Mayall, et al. (Western, 1985), *Starwatch* by Ben Mayer (Longmeadow Press, 1984), *The Space Atlas* by Heather Couper and Nigel Henbest (Gulliver/Harcourt, 1992), and *About Stars and Planets* by James Muirden (Franklin Watts, 1987).

Jane Yolen Wrote:

Briar Rose

Cards of Grief

Children of the Wolf

The Devil's Arithmetic

Dragons & Dreams

Encounter

The Gift of Sarah Barker

The Pit Dragon Trilogy

2041: Twelve Short Stories About the Future

Wizard's Hall

Good Versus Evil

Cooper, Susan. The Dark Is Rising series

LeGuin, Ursula. The Earthsea Trilogy

L'Engle, Madeleine. The Time Trilogy

Yep, Laurence. Dragon Cauldron

———. Dragon of the Lost Sea

———. Dragon Steel

Yolen, Jane. Wizard's Hall

Wizards

Baum, Frank L. The Wizard of Oz

Duane, Diane. So You Want to Be a Wizard?

Hansen, Ron. The Shadowmaker

Kisling, Lee. The Fool's War

MacLachlan, Patricia. Tomorrow's Wizard

Manning-Sanders, Ruth. A Book of Wizards

Pierce, Tamora. Alanna: The First Adventure

Tannen, Mary. The Wizard Children of Finn

Ure, Jean. The Wizard in the Woods

Yolen, Jane. Wizard's Hall

Rip-Roaring Reads
for
High School Students

Bennett, Jay
Coverup

LC 91-18506, ©1991, 144p., $13.90 (ISBN 0-531-15224-3; ISBN 0-531-11091-5, library binding), Franklin Watts. Paperback $3.99 (ISBN 0-449-70409-2), Fawcett Juniper

Genres: Contemporary realistic fiction, mystery

Themes: Alcohol abuse, hit-and-run drivers, friendship, truth, corruption, drunken driving, accidents, responsibility, torment, deceit, the homeless, romance, investigation

Reading level: Fifth grade

Interest level: Seventh through twelfth grades

Reviews:
Booklist. 88(5):505 November 1, 1991
School Library Journal. 37(8):195 August, 1991
Voice of Youth Advocates. 14(4):222 October, 1991. (#4 quality, #4 popularity)

Author Information
Born in New York City in 1912, Jay Bennett began writing at the age of eighteen. He struggled for over fourteen years to be published. His career was finally launched when a radio drama he wrote was accepted. Since then he has written for radio and television. After writing several adult mysteries, Bennett discovered the young adult field and has been writing mysteries for this group ever since. He was the first writer to win the prestigious Edgar Award for Juvenile Mysteries two years in a row. Bennett says he continues to write for young adults partly because he himself is a kid who has never grown up, but mostly because he has strong feelings about young adults. He says, "It's up to the young to help turn things around."

Plot Summary
The morning after a wild party finds Brad with a hazy recollection of a car accident. The driver, who is Brad's best friend, Alden, insists that nothing happened. Despite Alden's continual denial, Brad is sure that something is being concealed. When the Judge, Alden's father, takes Brad aside and insists he drop the subject, Brad becomes determined to find the truth.

Introducing the Book
Short chapters and a terse voice make this quick read a surefire winner. Read aloud to the bottom of page 18 (seven actual pages of text) to hook potential readers. The topical subject and Bennett's style make this book zoom along. *Coverup* appeared on the 1992 ALA/YALSA Recommended Books for the Reluctant Young Adult Reader list.

Booktalks

In the Aisle
Too much to drink at the party and a confusing and barely remembered ride home. Why is Brad so certain that something terrible has happened? His friend Alden, the driver, insists everything is all right, but Brad's mind will not let him rest. He is certain that something is being covered up.

With the Author's Words
Returning to the scene of the crime, Brad is determined to find evidence of an accident he is sure happened the night before.

> *There must be something left here.... Bits of headlight glass. Some spots of dried blood. Shreds of ripped clothing. A button torn off a jacket. He slowly straightened up and stood in the darkness thinking, his face grim and white. There was nothing. It was as if someone had come and swept the road and its sides clean. Not a trace of anything. Who could have done it? And why? And the body?* (P. 38, hardback edition)

What body? What accident? Why is Brad so certain there is a *coverup?*

Literature Extensions/Alternative Book Report Activities

Economics/Agricultural Subsidies—Ellen's father is homeless because his farm failed and he was left without a home or a job. The plight of American farmers is addressed in current literature. Students can research this topical issue and also consult *America's Farm Crisis* by Carol Gorman (Franklin Watts, 1987), *Farm: A Year in the Life of an American Farmer* by Richard Rhodes (Simon & Schuster, 1989), *The Politics of Food: The Decline of Agriculture and the Rise of Agribusiness in America* by Joel Solkoff (Sierra Club Books, 1985), and *The Embattled Farmer* by Jay Staten and Pat Staten (Fulcrum, 1987).

Government/Corruption—Alden's father, the Judge, is in a position to influence local law officers, and he uses his power to cover up the crime Alden commits. Use this as a springboard for further research into political corruption, for example, the savings and loan scandal, the Iran-Contra affair, Watergate, the Teapot Dome scandal, and so on.

Consult *The Whistleblowers: Exposing Corruption in Government and Industry* by Myron Peretz Glazer and Penina Migdal (Basic Books, 1989), *American Political Scandals Past and Present* by Barbara Silberdick Feinberg (Franklin Watts, 1992), *Essentials of Government Ethics* edited by Peter Madsen and Jay M. Shafritz (Plume Books, 1992), or *Famous Presidential Scandals* by Don Lawson (Enslow, 1990).

Health—Bennett addresses teen alcohol abuse and the issue of drunken driving. With the ever-changing adolescent population, the need to address these issues is ongoing.

Make available some of the many titles on this subject such as *Contract for Life* by Robert Anastas (Pocket Books, 1986), Paul Dolmetsch and Gail Mauricette's *Teen Talk About Alcohol and Alcoholism* (Dolphin Books, 1987), Jane Claypool Miner's *Alcohol and You* (Franklin Watts, 1988), *Straight Talk About Drinking: Teenagers Speak out About Alcohol* by Wayne Coffey (New American Library, 1988), *Drinking, Driving & Drugs* by Jean McBee Knox (Chelsea House, 1988), and *Driving the Drunk off the Road: A Handbook for Action* by Sandy Golden (Quince Mill Books, 1983).

Related videos are *It Won't Happen to Me* (Coronet/MTI Films & Video) and *Don't Say Yes When You Really Mean No* (Magic Music).

Social Issues/Community—The victim of the hit-and-run in *Coverup* was a homeless man. What services does your community provide for the homeless? Can your class help by collecting clothes, raising money, serving food, and so on?

For further information, refer students to *The Fight Against Homelessness* by Margaret Fagan (Franklin Watts, 1990), *The Homeless* by Laurie Beckelman (Macmillan, 1989), *The Homeless: Opposing Viewpoints* by Lisa Orr (Greenhaven Press, 1990), and *The Place I Call Home: The Faces and Voices of Homeless Teens* by Lois Stavsky and I. E. Mozeson (Shapolsky, 1991).

Jay Bennett Wrote:

Coverup

The Dark Corridor

The Death Ticket

Deathman, Don't Follow Me

The Executioner

The Haunted One

I Never Said I Loved You

Instruments of Darkness

The Killing Tree

The Long Black Coat

Nightmare Town

Say Hello to the Hit Man

Sing Me a Death Song

The Skeleton Man

Alone and Coping

Bennett, Jay. *Coverup*

Brooks, Bruce. *The Moves Make the Man*

Hamilton, Virginia. *Sweet Whispers, Brother Rush*

Hinton, S. E. *The Outsiders*

Korman, Gordon. *Losing Joe's Place*

Peck, Richard. *Are You In the House Alone?*

Spinelli, Jerry. *Maniac Magee*

Taylor, Theodore. *Sniper*

Wyss, Thelma Hatch. *Here at the Scenic-Vu Motel*

Drinking and Driving Novels

Bennett, Jay. *Coverup*

Bunting, Eve. *A Sudden Silence*

Duder, Tessa. *In Lane Three, Alex Archer*

Forman, James D. *The Big Bang*

Harrell, Janice. *Flashpoint*

Kropp, Paul. *Death Ride*

Peck, Richard. *I Know What You Did Last Summer*

Pike, Christopher. *Chain Letter*

Starkman, Neal. *The Apple*

Strasser, Todd. *The Accident*

Voigt, Cynthia. *Izzy, Willy-Nilly*

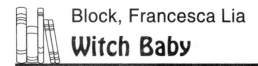

Block, Francesca Lia
Witch Baby

LC 90-28916, ©1991, 103p., $13.89 (ISBN 0-06-020547-4; ISBN 0-06-020548-2, library binding), HarperCollins. Paperback $3.95 (ISBN 0-0-06-447065-2), Harper Trophy

Genre: Contemporary realistic fiction, multicultural

Themes: Blended families, belonging, coming of age, love, loneliness, abandonment, acceptance, differences, interracial relations, compassion, homosexuality, tolerance, immigration, jealousy, truth, music, running away

Reading level: Fifth grade

Interest level: Eighth through twelfth grades

Reviews:
Bulletin of the Center for Children's Books.
    45(2):31 October, 1991. (Recommended)
Horn Book. 68(1):78-79 January/February,
    1992
School Library Journal. 37(9):277 September,
    1991. (Starred)
Voice of Youth Advocates. 14(5):305 December, 1991. (#5 quality, #5 popularity)

Author Information
A Los Angeles resident, Francesca Lia Block graduated from the University of California at Berkeley in 1986. Encouraged by her parents, Block began to write at an early age. Poetry has always been important to her; she appreciates the deep emotion reflected in that literature form. Block says her style is a "kind of magic realism." A continuing theme in her work is the confrontation of darkness with a strong belief in the magic of love and art.

Plot Summary
Witch Baby lives with an unusual extended family in the Los Angeles area. She tries to come to grips with her place in the family while despairing over the woes of the world. After Witch Baby finally meets her birth mother, she is able to accept the love of her "real" family.

Introducing the Book
This sequel to *Weetzie Bat* (HarperCollins, 1989) is an unusual book in terms of style, characterization, names, use of slang, and so on. It is almost surreal but has the potential to capture teen readers because of its honest, lyrical, and offbeat style. Some reviews liken this book to a rock music video, and indeed music plays an important part in the story. Consider playing reggae music or music by Los Lobos (a Los Angeles barrio band) as part of the introduction. Read aloud to page 15 (hardback edition), ending with "He carried it over to Witch Baby and placed it in her arms." Read slowly to allow listeners an opportunity to visualize the unusual names and the characters they portray. A third book in the series is *Cherokee Bat and the Goat Guys* (HarperCollins, 1992). *Witch Baby* was included on the 1992 ALA/YALSA Recommended Books for the Reluctant Young Adult Reader list.

Booktalks

In the Aisle
Witch Baby is the name (really) of the girl in this book. She's looking for lots of things—her real family, her own boyfriend, and peace and harmony in the world. Her search has her roller-skating through parts of L.A. and stowing away in car trunks. Witch Baby speaks the truth no one wants to hear. Will you listen?

With the Author's Words

Witch Baby will tug at your heartstrings as she desperately searches for her rightful place in her family.

> *Witch Baby was wild, snarled, tangled and angry. Everyone got more and more frustrated with her. When they tried to grab her, even for a hug, she would wriggle away, her body quick-slippery as a fish. She never cried, but she always wanted to cry.* (P. 26, hardback edition)

Travel with Witch Baby as she runs away, pounds on her drums, and watches her half-sister steal her boyfriend. Do witch babies ever cry?

Literature Extensions/Alternative Book Report Activities

Health—Witch Baby's nontraditional family includes gay lovers Dirk and Duck. This book can be used in conjunction with a unit on safe sex, because that is strongly advocated in Block's novel.

Provide other current books such as *The Complete Guide to Safe Sex* by Ted McIlvenna et al. (Specific Press, 1987), *Safe Sex: What Everyone Should Know About Sexually Transmitted Diseases* by Angelo T. Scotti and Thomas A. Moore (PaperJacks, 1987), *Safe Sex in a Dangerous World* by Art Ulene (Random House, 1987), *Tell It Like It Is: Straight Talk About Sex* by Annamaria Formichella et al. (Avon Books, 1991), *100 Questions and Answers About AIDS: A Guide for Young People* by Michael Thomas Ford (Macmillan, 1991), *Be Smart About Sex* by Jean Fiedler and Hal Fiedler (Enslow, 1990), and *What You Can Do to Avoid AIDS* by Earvin "Magic" Johnson (Times Books, 1992).

A related video is *Double Dutch—Double Jeopardy* (Durrin Productions).

Journalism—Witch Baby routinely cuts articles from the newspaper about "nuclear accidents, violence, poverty and disease." Using a variety of newspapers, journalism students can select articles on a specific theme as preparation for writing their own articles.

Photography—Witch Baby chronicles the life of her "almost family" through photographs. Choosing an event or subject, students can photograph a sequence of scenes for display or publication. Students can also learn film processing and developing techniques in conjunction with this project.

Video/Movie Making—Witch Baby's family is involved in filmmaking. They produce movies that make a difference about important issues and events. Using school or public access video equipment, students can write, shoot, and produce a video on an issue central to their lives.

Refer to *Make Your Own Music Video* by James B. Meigs and Jennifer A. Stern (Franklin Watts, 1986), *How to Make Your Own Video* by Perry Schwartz (Lerner, 1991), *Make Your Own Animated Movies and Videotapes* by Yvonne Andersen (Little, Brown, 1991), and *Video Power: A Complete Guide to Writing, Planning and Shooting Videos* by Tom Shachtman and Harriet Shelare (Holt, Rinehart & Winston, 1988).

Peace

Durrell, Ann. *The Big Book for Peace*

Fry-Miller, Kathleen. *Young Peacemakers Project Book*

Hye, Naomi Shihab. *This Same Sky: A Selection of Poems*

MacDonald, Margaret Read. *Peace Tales: World Folktales to Tale About*

Meltzer, Milton. *Ain't Gonna Study War No More: The Story of America's Peace Seekers*

Phillips, Ann. *The Peace Child*

Scholes, Katherine. *Peace Begins with You*

Seeley, Robert A. *The Handbook of Non-violence*

Belonging

Block, Francesca Lia. *Cherokee Bat and the Goat Guys*

——. *Weetzie Bat*

——. *Witch Baby*

Cannon, A. E. *Cal Cameron by Day, Spider Man by Night*

Cooney, Caroline B. *The Face on the Milk Carton*

Froehlich, Margaret. *Reasons to Stay*

Mazer, Harry. *City Light*

Plummer, Louise. *My Name is Sus5an Smith. The 5 is Silent*

Power of Photography: The Visions of Four Artists

Alinder, James, and John Szarkowski. *Ansel Adams: Classic Images*

Daffron, Carolyn. *Margaret Bourke-White*

Meltzer, Milton. *Dorothea Lange: Life Through the Camera*

Parks, Gordon. *Voices in the Mirror: An Autobiography*

Bradbury, Ray
The Ray Bradbury Chronicles, Volume 1

LC 92-2979, ©1992, 77p., $10.00 (ISBN 0-553-35125-7), Bantam Books

Illustrated by Dave Gibbons et al.

Genres: Graphic novel (comic book or trade comic), science fiction, fantasy

Themes: Space travel, Mars, robots, genetics, environment, time travel, the future, the sun, dinosaurs, dragons, trains

Reading level: Sixth grade

Interest level: Seventh through twelfth grades

Author Information

Born in 1920, Ray Bradbury has been writing and publishing since 1942. As a child he loved comic books and comic strips, and his writing has been greatly influenced by science fiction magazines and movies. When he was fourteen his family moved to Los Angeles and Bradbury became entranced with the movies. His writing career began when he sold a few short stories to science fiction magazines. To date, Bradbury has published over 300 short stories, and he says he has written 2,000. Bradbury has achieved stature as a writer of short stories, novels, plays, screenplays, and poetry. He writes and reads poetry nearly every day.

Plot Summary

Six authorized, adapted, and illustrated stories are taken from the vast writings of Ray Bradbury. The volume is introduced by Bradbury himself and includes short notes preceding each story. The chronicles include stories featuring the colonization of Mars, a voyage to the sun, robots, time travel, a surprise, and an abandoned rocket.

Introducing the Book

The comic book format of this book will attract even the most reluctant reader. Students who like science fiction and heavily illustrated works will eagerly pick this up. Volumes 2 and 3 will keep them reading, and there are plenty of Ray Bradbury titles available for further delving.

Booktalks

In the Aisle

Join Ray Bradbury as these comic book illustrators adapt and illustrate six of his stories. Read these to find out if earthmen can become aliens, if an ancient myth can become reality, what dragons are made of, whether robots develop their own personalities, and if you can change the future.

With the Author's Words

Braling will do almost anything for some time away from his wife. After all, she coerced him into marriage ten years before and ever since then has kept him from going out at night. When Braling discovers Marionettes, Inc., can make duplicates, he signs up. Explaining his newfound freedom to a friend, Braling tells how he got away from his wife.

> I went down to the cellar, took Braling Two out of his box, and sent him back up to sit with my wife, while I came out to see you!... He's made to last for six months, if necessary. He'll eat, sleep, perspire.... Everything as natural as can be. You'll take good care of my wife, won't you, Braling Two? (P. 3 of "Marionettes, Inc.")

Braling Two is most accommodating. In fact, he grows quite fond of Braling's wife and dislikes the metal box in the cellar. This is just one of the chronicles in this comic book version of Ray Bradbury stories, and if you like this, you'll love the others!

Literature Extensions/Alternative Book Report Activities

Art—In the story "Dark They Were and Golden Eyed," Earth colonizers on Mars speculate about the Martian paintings located in the ruins: "You see Martian paintings and you wonder what the painter was like. You make a little ghost in your mind, a memory. It's quite natural. Imagination." "You haven't been prowling up in those ruins, have you?" (P. 14)

Have students use their imaginations. What do Martian paintings look like? Present the completed works in a Mars Art Gallery. Some students with architectural interests may like to construct a Martian home to compare with the Earthlings' homes on Mars.

Creative Writing—The story "Marionettes, Inc." is a cautionary tale about a man escaping from his wife by leaving a robot in his place. If you replaced yourself with a robot, where would the real you go? What would the real you do? Students can write a poem, essay, or short story depicting events that transpire after they have been replaced by robots.

Literature/Writing—The stories included in *Chronicles 1* were all original Bradbury stories that have been adapted to the graphic novel format. Create a classroom library of original Bradbury works. Many of the books listed below were adapted in this graphic novel collection.

Include *Fahrenheit 451* (Ballentine Books, 1981), *The Illustrated Man* (Doubleday, 1951), *The Martian Chronicles* (Doubleday, 1958), *The Golden Apples of the Sun* (Granada, 1977), *R Is for Rocket* (Doubleday, 1962), *Something Wicked This Way Comes* (Bantam Books, 1963), *The Stories of Ray Bradbury* (Alfred A. Knopf, 1980), *The Toynbee Convector and Other Stories* (Random House, 1988): and *A Graveyard for Lunatics: Another Tale of Two Cities* (Alfred A. Knopf, 1990).

Bradbury's *Zen in the Art of Writing: Essays on Creativity* (Capra Press, 1990) includes information about writing as Bradbury looks at his own body of work.

Media—In the introduction to *Chronicles 1*, Bradbury mentions several movies he was involved with. Provide the following films (a good video store will have them in stock) for a Ray Bradbury film festival: *The Lost World* (TCF/Saratoca, 1960), *King Kong* (RKO, 1933), *The Beast From 20,000 Fathoms* (Warner, 1953), *Mighty Joe Young* (RKO, 1949), and *Moby Dick* (John Huston, 1956).

Ray Bradbury Wrote:

Fahrenheit 451

The Golden Apples of the Sun

A Graveyard for Lunatics: Another Tale of Two Cities

The Illustrated Man

The Martian Chronicles

R Is for Rocket

Something Wicked This Way Comes

Science Fiction

Adams, Douglas. *The Hitchhiker's Guide to the Galaxy*

Baird, Thomas. *Smart Rats*

Hughes, Monica. *Devil on My Back*

——. *Invitation to the Game*

Macklin, Ken. *Dr. Watchstop: Adventures in Time and Space*

Sleator, William. *The Duplicator*

——. *The Green Futures of Tycho*

Williams, Shelia, and Charles Ardai, eds. *Why I Left Harry's All-Night Hamburgers: And Other Stories from Isaac Asimov's Science Fiction Magazine*

Graphic Novel— A longer and more sophisticated version of a comic book.

These self-contained stories use text and artwork to advance the plot and set new visual standards. These longer short stories or short novels are usually the size of a magazine.

Bradbury, Ray. *Chronicles 1*

——. *Chronicles 2*

Doyle, Sir Arthur Conan. *Sherlock Holmes: A Study in Scarlet*

Eisner, Will. *The Dreamer*

Jean-Philippe, Claude, and Patrick Lesueur. *Bogie*

Pini, Wendy, and Richard Pini. *The Elfquest series*

Pratt, George. *Enemy Ace*

Spiegleman, Art. *Maus*

——. *Maus II*

Wildey, Doug. *Rio*

Cohen, Daniel
Ghostly Tales of Love & Revenge

LC 91-37957, ©1992, 95p., $14.95 (ISBN 0-399-22117-4), Putnam

Genres: Supernatural, short story, folktale

Themes: Ghosts, love, revenge, death, evil spirits, despair, loneliness, abandonment, mourning, accidents, warnings, fate

Reading level: Sixth grade

Interest level: Fifth through twelfth grades

Reviews:
Booklist. 88(22):2003 August, 1992
School Library Journal. 38(7):72 July, 1992
Voice of Youth Advocates. 15(4):250 October, 1992. (#4 quality, #5 popularity)

Author Information
As a teenager, Daniel Cohen was fascinated with the bizarre. An avid science fiction reader, he also loved reading about sea monsters, dragons, and UFOs. For ten years Cohen contributed to *Science Digest*, writing popular science articles. However, he discovered that the most popular articles were those on more unusual topics like UFOs and ESP. Cohen's first book was a collection of his *Science Digest* articles, and since then he has written over a hundred books. When Cohen finds an interesting subject, he enjoys learning more about it as he writes it all down. Cohen connects with readers who may not ordinarily read for pleasure but pick up his books because they are fascinated with the subject matter. His collections of ghost stories come from many sources but never from his own imagination. Instead he deals with factual and semifactual accounts as well as legends. Cohen notes that telling ghost stories is one of the oldest forms of entertainment.

Plot Summary
This collection of thirteen ghostly tales focuses on the themes of love and revenge. The stories come from folktales and legends that may or may not be true, but have been passed on through generations from worldwide locales.

Introducing the Book
Taking little selling, this short, fascinating collection can be introduced by reading aloud the two-page introduction or the second story in chapter 4, "Two Japanese Tales," or both. The themes of ghosts and love make this a surefire winner for all readers

Booktalks

In the Aisle
Is love stronger than death? The stories from *Ghostly Tales of Love & Revenge* come from around the world and from the grave. Some of these ghosts are searching for their true loves, while others simply want revenge. Leave the light on!

With the Author's Words
When Robert Stuart made plans to return to his native Scotland, he knew he was leaving behind a woman who was obsessed with him. He thought he could sneak away, but she appeared just as he was leaving.

> *"You shan't go!" she shrieked. "I tell you this, Robert Stuart—if you marry any woman but me I shall come between you to the end of your days!" She then grabbed hold of the front wheel of the coach to prevent it from starting. "Drive on! Drive on!" shouted Stuart. The driver obeyed. As the wheels began to turn the girl fell directly in front of the carriage. She screamed as the wheel went over her forehead.* (Pp. 14-15, hardback edition)

Robert may think he has seen the last of poor Jeanne. This is a story of love and more: it's a story of Jeanne's ghostly revenge. How does she do it? Cohen tells her story and others in *Ghostly Tales of Love & Revenge.*

Literature Extensions/Alternative Book Report Activities

Art—Using the vivid descriptions of the ghosts in Cohen's collection, students can sketch, draw, or paint the characters to create a Gallery of Ghosts. Decorate your room or school, or use the creepy portraits in the haunted house activity below. For inspiration consult *Draw 50 Monsters, Creeps, Superheroes, Demons, Dragons, Nerds, Dirts, Ghouls, Giants, Vampires, Zombies, and Other Curiosa...* by Lee J. Ames (Doubleday, 1983).

Extracurricular Activities/Fund-Raisers/Haunted Houses—Using the artwork described above, plus created haunts based on Cohen's thirteen short stories, build a "haunted house" for a club fund-raiser or as a service project for a community activity. For additional information consult *How to Haunt a House for Halloween* by the magician Robert Friedhoffer (Franklin Watts, 1988), or *How to Operate a Financially Successful Haunted House* by Philip Morris and Dennis Phillips (Imagine, 1967).

Journalism/Investigative Reporting—As exemplified by Cohen's collection, nearly every culture and locale has its own ghostly tales. Using primary sources, such as interviews, and newspaper research, students can uncover local ghosts and their origins.

Research/The Paranormal—Cohen refers to paranormal investigator Elliott O'Donnell in the short story "Pearlin Jean." Other such investigators have explored haunted houses and ghostly occurrences and written about their experiences. Develop a classroom library for interested students.

Books included might be *The Moving Coffins: Ghosts and Hauntings Around the World* by David C. Knight (Prentice-Hall, 1987), *Southern Ghosts* by Nancy Roberts (Sandlapper Press, 1979), *Best True Ghost Stories* by Hans Holzer (Prentice-Hall, 1986), *The Haunted Realm: Ghosts, Spirits and Their Uncanny Abodes* by Simon Marsden (Dutton, 1987), *The Encyclopedia of Ghosts and Spirits* by Rosemary Ellen Guiley (Facts on File, 1992), and *The Screaming Skull* by William E. Warren (Prentice-Hall, 1987).

Daniel Cohen Wrote:

Ghostly Tales of Love & Revenge

The Ghosts of War

Phantom Animals

Phone Call from a Ghost

Prophets of Doom

Railway Ghosts and Highway Horrors

Southern Fried Rat and Other Gruesome Tales

Quick Reads—Thin Books

Block, Francesca Lia. Weetzie Bat

Clavell, James. The Children's Story

Cohen, Daniel. Ghostly Tales of Love & Revenge

Cormier, Robert. Tunes for Bears to Dance To

Fleischman, Paul. The Borning Room

Knudson, R. R. Rinehart Lifts

Paulsen, Gary. Nightjohn

———. Popcorn Days & Buttermilk Nights

Rylant, Cynthia. A Couple of Kooks and Other Stories About Love

Love to Be Scared

Aiken, Joan. A Foot in the Grave

Alcock, Vivien. Ghostly Companions: A Feast of Chilling Tales

Cohen, Daniel. Ghostly Tales of Love & Revenge

———. Railway Ghosts and Highway Horrors

Henry, Maeve. A Gift for a Gift; A Ghost Story

Jacques, Brian. Seven Strange & Ghostly Tales

McDonald, Collin. Nightwaves: Scary Tales for After Dark

McKissack, Patricia C. The Dark-Thirty: Southern Tales of the Supernatural

Nixon, Joan Lowery. Secret, Silent Screams

———. Whispers of the Dead

Notze, Sollace. Acquainted with the Night

Westwood, Chris. Shock Waves

Wilson, Colin. The Mammoth Book of the Supernatural

Crutcher, Chris
Athletic Shorts: Six Short Stories

LC 91-4418, ©1989, 1991, 154p., $13.95 (ISBN 0-688-10816-4), Greenwillow Books. Paperback $3.50 (ISBN 0-440-21390-8), Dell

Genres: Contemporary realistic fiction, short story

Themes: Athletics, self-esteem, coming of age, father-son relationships, love, memories, death, friendship, homosexuality, hate, racism, AIDS, truth, boy-girl relationships, anger, forgiveness, cruelty, insecurity

Reading level: Sixth grade

Interest level: Eighth through twelfth grades

Reviews:
Booklist. 88(4):428 October 15, 1991
Bulletin of the Center for Children's Books. 45(4):87 December, 1991. (Advised)
Horn Book. 62(5):602-03 September/October, 1991. (Starred)
School Library Journal. 37(9):278 September, 1991. (Starred)
Voice of Youth Advocates. 15(1):26 April, 1992. (#5 quality, #4 popularity)

Author Information
Chris Crutcher grew up in a small logging town in northern Idaho. Despite, or in spite of, his bookish parents, Crutcher read only one book throughout four years of high school. That novel was *To Kill a Mockingbird* by Harper Lee, and its treatment of justice and real life greatly influenced Crutcher's writing. After completing college at Eastern Washington State College, where he spent more time swimming than on his majors of sociology and psychology, Crutcher taught in an alternative school in California. That experience is related in *The Crazy Horse Electric Game.* After ten years of urban life and standing in lines, Crutcher returned to the Northwest. He settled in Spokane, Washington, and is currently a child and family therapist specializing in families involved with child abuse. Crutcher hopes his books reflect his fervent belief in basic connections that exist among all people and what he calls the "true nature of courage." He has had little formal writing training; his style comes from personal experiences. Crutcher says he sees writing as a method of expressing humor and a way to "present different human perspectives."

Plot Summary
These six short stories feature many characters who have previously appeared in Crutcher's books. Though the characters are athletes, the stories aren't centered on their athletic achievements but focus instead on individual courage and truth seeking. Crutcher's ability to realistically and honestly portray human beings with all their foibles as well as their humor gives the reader a broader insight into people. This book's included on the 1992 ALA/YALSA Recommended Books for the Reluctant Young Adult Reader list.

Introducing the Book
Use this book to introduce the short story genre. Read aloud "The Other Pin" (Pp. 55-80, hardback edition) to hook both male and female readers; it's the only story in this collection with a strong female character and it includes fewer sensitive issues. Be sure to make Crutcher's novels available because most of the short stories are continuations of or prequels to these works.

Booktalks

In the Aisle
Most kids don't think that things like AIDS, homosexuality, and death will ever touch their lives, but these athletes in Crutcher's short stories find out differently. These are stories about love and death, about laughter and pain. They are about people just like you.

With the Author's Words

Meet Lionel Serbousek whose parents were killed in a boating accident when he was fourteen years old. Lionel is haunted by his memories of that day and often wonders what might have been.

> *My name is Lionel Serbousek. I'm a high school senior, an artist and a swimmer, and I like to think, finally, a good friend. I'm also an orphan; I live by myself. I can tell no story about my life without telling this one first because it colors everything I do and everything I think.* (P. 85, hardback edition)

In that boating accident, Lionel lost more than his parents, he lost a piece of himself. How he works it all out is told in "Goin' Fishin?"—one of the short stories in Chris Crutcher's *Athletic Shorts*.

Literature Extensions/Alternative Book Report Activities

Creative Writing/Literary Devices—In Crutcher's story "Goin' Fishin'," Lionel says, "Fishing was a metaphor for life with my father" (Pp. 88, hardback edition). Students can write their own stories using metaphors. Some examples include football, skiing, mountain climbing, cooking, gardening, or simply walking down the street.

Creative Writing/Short Stories—Most of the stories in *Athletic Shorts* are extensions of characters Crutcher previously wrote about in novels (see bookmark #3). Consult the foreword in *Athletic Shorts*, pages 1-2, for more specific information. Have students select a character from any favorite novel and write a continuation in short story format.

Health/AIDS—One of Crutcher's characters faces death by AIDS. Keep students informed about new information on this disease and its potential effect on their lives. Provide current materials such as *Teens with AIDS Speak Out* by Mary Kittredge (Messner, 1992), *Risky Times: How to Be AIDS-Smart and Stay Healthy* by Jeanne Blake (Workman, 1990), *AIDS* by Stephen A. Flanders and Carl N. Flanders (Facts on File, 1991), *100 Questions and Answers About AIDS: A Guide for Young People* by Michael Thomas Ford (Macmillan, 1992), *What You Can Do to Avoid AIDS* by Earvin "Magic" Johnson (Times Books, 1992), *AIDS Issues: A Handbook* by David E. Newton (Enslow, 1992), and *The AIDS Acquired Immunodeficiency Syndrome Handbook: A Complete Guide to Education and Awareness* by Brenda S. Faison and Laila Moustafa (Designbase, 1991).

Consult *Facts on File* and *Readers' Guide to Periodical Literature* for up-to-date information, because new drugs, therapy, and scientific developments are continually changing the AIDS situation. *Book Links* 2(2): 11-15, November, 1992, pages 11-15, provides a bibliography on HIV and AIDS for books, videos, adult resource and national organization addresses.

A topical video is *Growing Up in the Age of AIDS* (MPI Video, 1992).

Sociology/Racism/Bigotry—Crutcher says that all of us are bigots and that we all prejudge on some basis (see paragraph 1 of the preface to "In the Time I Get," P. 127, hardback edition). In the preface to "Telephone Man," Crutcher addresses the topic of racism (P. 107, hardback edition). These two related topics can be discussed in conjunction with these short stories and other contemporary works as well.

Provide students with novels such as Chris Reaves's *Mote* (Delacorte Press, 1990), Jay Bennett's *Skinhead* (Franklin Watts, 1991), and Marie G. Lee's *Finding My Voice* (Houghton Mifflin, 1992); and nonfiction works like James Aho's *Politics of Righteousness: Idaho Christian Patriotism* (University of Washington Press, 1990), *Two Nations: Black and White, Separate, Hostile, Unequal* by Andrew Hacker (Scribners, 1992), Michael Kronenwetter's *United They Hate: White Supremacists in America* (Walker, 1992) and *Taking a Stand Against Human Rights Abuses* (Franklin Watts, 1990), and *Racism in America: Opposing Viewpoints* by William Dudley and Charles Cozic (Greenhaven Press, 1991) for background information. A related video is *Skin* (Landmark Films).

Stage a classroom or all-school dialogue or debate to discuss racism and bigotry as they occur in your school or community.

Read More About Them: Characters from *Athletic Shorts* by Chris Crutcher

The Crazy Horse Electric Game, with characters from "Telephone Man," "The Pin," and "The Other Pin"

Running Loose, with characters from "In the Time I Get"

Stotan! with characters from "Goin' Fishin'"

Other Crutcher Books:

Chinese Handcuffs

The Deep End: A Novel of Suspense

Teen Novels: The Issue Is Gays and Lesbians

Block, Francesca Lia. *Weetzie Bat*

———. *Witch Baby*

Garden, Nancy. *Annie on My Mind*

Hall, Richard. *Family Fictions*

Holland, Isabelle. *The Man Without a Face*

Homes, A. M. *Jack*

Kerr, M. E. *Nightkites*

Klein, Norma. *My Life as a Body*

Koertge, Ron. *The Arizona Kid*

Shannon, George. *Unlived Affections*

Siman, Ken. *Pizza Face: Or, The Hero of Suburbia*

Sweeney, Joyce. *Face the Dragon*

Wersba, Barbara. *Crazy Vanilla*

Short Stories for Teens

Beattie, Ann. *Distortions*

Benard, Robert, ed. *All Problems Are Simple and Other Stories*

Cormier, Robert. *Eight Plus One*

Gale, David, ed. *Funny You Should Ask: The Delacorte Book of Original Humorous Short Stories*

Gallo, Donald R., ed. *Connections*

Gingher, Marianne. *Teen Angel: And Other Stories of Young Love*

Gold, Ron, ed. *Stepping Stones*

Rylant, Cynthia. *A Couple of Kooks and Other Stories About Love*

Sieruta, Peter D. *Heartbeats and Other Stories*

Updike, David. *Out on the Marsh*

Wilson, Budge. *The Leaving*

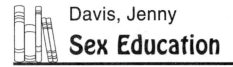

Davis, Jenny
Sex Education

LC 87-30441, ©1988, 150p., $13.95 (ISBN 0-531-05756-9; ISBN 0-531-08356-X, library binding), Orchard Books. Paperback $2.95 (ISBN 0-440-20483-6), Dell

Genre: Contemporary realistic fiction

Themes: Sex education, caring, compassion, value of self, teenage pregnancy, school life, friendship, boy-girl relationships, domestic violence, mental health, courage, death, justice, denial

Readability: Fifth grade

Interest Level: Ninth through twelfth grades

Reviews:
Booklist. 85(1):68. September 1, 1988. (Starred)
School Library Journal. 35(1):197 September, 1988. (Starred)
Voice Of Youth Advocates. 11(3):130 August, 1988. (#4 quality, #5 popularity)

Author Information
Jenny Davis lives in Lexington, Kentucky, with her two sons. She teaches sex education and English at Lexington School. Davis is very attached to teens and loves to read young adult literature as well as write it. *Sex Education* is her second novel. Davis says she was compelled to tell the story of David and Livvie because they "perched on her shoulder" and insisted. It was a difficult novel for her to write, she says.

Plot Summary
Told in flashback, journal style, and written in a psychiatric hospital, this is the story of Livvie and her boyfriend, David. They are ninth-graders taking a biology class from a nontraditional teacher who abandons the regular curriculum to teach a unit on sex education, focusing on caring for one's self and compassion for others. Livvie and David become very close as they share a "caring project" for a new neighbor, a victim of domestic violence. *Sex Education* was included on the 1989 ALA/YALSA Recommended Books for the Reluctant Young Adult Reader list.

Introducing the Book
No teenager should miss reading this book—independently. Sensitive subject matter and some language might make this difficult to share aloud past page 15. Be sure to booktalk it; the title alone will sell it. To firmly hook readers, read aloud the four-page prologue.

Booktalks

In the Aisle
Do you like books with caring, romance, and plenty of suspense? *Sex Education* is about two high school kids named Livvie and David who choose a lonely new neighbor, Maggie, as the subject of a "caring project" for biology class. Because her husband always seems so grumpy and mean, they sneak to her house to visit when he's away. This might remind you of "Beauty and the Beast," except Maggie's husband turns out to be more than just a beast; he is dangerous!

With the Author's Words
This is supposed to be biology class, but Mrs. Fulton, the teacher, says she'll teach sex education instead. It is almost the end of the first class, and she still hasn't given the students their textbooks.

> *Most people knew who she was, but she'd never introduced herself or done any of the usual first day things. "For homework tonight," she said and then waited until the boos died down, "think about what sex is." "We will, we will," somebody called out. She laughed. "I'm sure you will. Remember, I said think. This is not hands-on homework. We'll talk about it tomorrow."* (Pp. 11-12, hardback edition)

This class will certainly be different. To attend, read Jenny Davis's *Sex Education*.

Literature Extensions/Alternative Book Report Activities

Communications/Advertising—In David and Livvie's sex education class, they discuss subliminal advertising and the use of sexual allusions to sell products. As an assignment, ask students to carefully observe television and print advertisements that use sex as a selling tool.

Refer to the following books for further information concerning subliminal advertising: *Subliminal Selling Skills* by Kerry L. Johnson (American Management Association, 1988), *The Want Makers: The World of Advertising: How They Make You Want to Buy* by Eric Clark (Viking, 1989), and *Caution! This May Be an Advertisement: A Teen Guide to Advertising* by Kathlyn Gay (Franklin Watts, 1992),

Community Service—Don't let what happens to Livvie and David discourage students from volunteering to help others. All communities have volunteer organizations with projects in which teenagers would be welcome volunteers. For example, many towns and cities sponsor paintfests in which local businesses provide materials and citizens provide the labor for refurbishing homes of the elderly and disabled.

Consult the *1992-1993 Directory of American Youth Organizations* compiled by Judith B. Erickson (Free Spirit, 1991), which is a guide to 500 clubs, groups, troops, teams, societies, and other organizations for young people; *People Who Make a Difference* by Brent Ashabranner (Dutton Children's Books, 1989); and *150 Ways Teens Can Make a Difference: A Handbook for Action* by Marian Salzman et al. (Peterson's Guides, 1991).

A national, nonprofit organization called StarServe provides free materials concerning community service for class and school projects. Request the StarServe education kit (also available in Spanish) and video resource guide from StarServe, Box 34567, Washington, DC 20043, 800-888-8232.

Health/Teen Pregnancy—What are the teen pregnancy statistics in your area? What services do your community and school district provide for teen parents and their offspring? Important books to make available include *Love & Sex & Growing Up* by Erick W. Johnson (Bantam Books, 1990) and *Girls and Sex and Boys and Sex,* 3rd edition, by Wardell B. Pomeroy, Ph.D. (Delacorte Press, 1991). Refer to the book entry for *What Do I Do Now?* (P. 105) for true-life experiences concerning teen parents and helpful reference books.

Health/Mental Health—Mental illness is often an avoided topic. Family members may feel embarrassed or guilty if they have relatives suffering from mental diseases. Refer to Sherry Dinner's *Nothing to Be Ashamed Of: Growing Up with Mental Illness in Your Family* (Lothrop, Lee & Shepard, 1989) and Julie Tallard Johnson's *Understanding Mental Illness: For Teens Who Care About Someone with Mental Illness* (Lerner, 1989).

Research—The media, such as books, magazines, and television movies, frequently cover the issue of abused women and their methods of retaliation or acquiescence. Research this topic using up-to-date articles found indexed in *Readers' Guide to Periodical Literature*. Some useful headings to search under include family violence and wife abuse.

♀ Sex Education ♂

Bell, Ruth, et al. *Changing Bodies, Changing Lives*

Benson, Michael D. *Coping with Birth Control*

Bernards, Neal, and Lynn Hall, eds. *Teenage Sexuality: Opposing Viewpoints*

Boston Children's Hospital. *What Teenagers Want to Know About Sex: Questions and Answers*

Boston Women's Health Book Collective. *The New Our Bodies, Ourselves*

Calderone, Mary S., and Eric W. Johnson. *The Family Book About Sexuality*

Fielder, Jean, and Hal Fiedler. *Be Smart About Sex: Facts for Young People*

Johanson, Sue. *Talk Sex*

Johnson, Eric W. *Love and Sex in Plain Language*

McCoy, Kathy, and Charles Wibbelsman. *The New Teenage Body Book*

Orr, Lisa, ed. *Sexual Values: Opposing Viewpoints*

Pomeroy, Wardell B. *Boys and Sex*

Voss, Jacqueline, and Jay Gale. *A Young Woman's Guide to Sex*

Caring

Casely, Judith. *Kisses*

Conrad, Pamela. *Holding Me Here*

Deaver, Julie R. *Say Goodnight, Gracey*

Klein, Norma. *Learning How to Fall*

Mango, Karin N. *Just for the Summer*

McKinley, Robin. *Beauty: A Retelling of the Story of Beauty and the Beast*

Neufeld, John. *Lisa, Bright and Dark*

Nixon, Joan Lowery. *The Other Side of Dark*

Oneal, Zibby. *The Language of Goldfish*

Rinaldi, Ann. *The Good Side of My Heart*

Talbert, Marc. *Rabbit in the Rock*

Woodson, Jacqueline. *The Dear One*

Dear Diary

Anon. *Go Ask Alice*

Avi. *Nothing But the Truth*

Hamm, Diane Johnston. *Bunkhouse Journal*

Harris, Marilyn. *The Runaway's Diary*

Keyes, Daniel. *Flowers for Algernon*

Marsden, John. *So Much to Tell You*

Orgel, Doris. *Risking Love*

Plath, Sylvia. *The Journals of Sylvia Plath*

Townsend, Sue. *The Adrian Mole Diaries*

Zindel, Paul. *The Amazing and Death Defying Diary of Eugene Dingman*

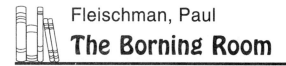

Fleischman, Paul
The Borning Room

LC 91-4432, ©1991, 101p., $13.89 (ISBN 0-06-023762-7; ISBN 0-06-0237785-6, library binding), HarperCollins

Genre: Historical fiction

Themes: Cycles of life, family life (1851-1918), superstitions, birth, death, farm life, grandfathers, inventions, runaway slaves, abolitionists, seances, suffragettes, community pressure, freedom of religion, war and peace, value of education

Reading level: Fifth grade

Interest level: Seventh grade and above

Reviews:
Booklist. 88(3):328 October 1, 1991. (Starred)
Bulletin of the Center for Children's Books. 45(1):9-10 September, 1991. (Recommended and starred)
Horn Book. 67(6):744-45 November/December, 1991. (Starred)
School Library Journal. 37(9):278 September, 1991. (Starred)
Voice of Youth Advocates. 14(5):310 December, 1991. (#5 quality, #3 popularity)

Author Information
Paul Fleischman is the son of children's author Sid Fleischman. He was born in California in 1952 and heard his father read his books aloud as he was writing them, chapter by chapter. Fleischman does most of his writing at a public library; he works with notebook and pencil, "very slowly and very carefully," he says. He attended the University of New Mexico and after graduating studied writing under his father. Paul Fleischman has always loved music and feels he would be writing music rather than books if he had the talent. He's worked as a bagel baker, a bookstore clerk, and a proofreader. Like his father, Fleischman is fascinated by history and loves to research historical names and places and facts about how people lived and worked in the past. He spends a good deal of time in used bookstores searching for information. Fleischman says, "You never know what you'll stumble onto in a book."

Plot Summary
The history of an Ohio farm family from 1851 to 1918 is revealed by Georgina as she reminisces about the borning room and its significance. She relates births and deaths against a background of the events during that period. Included are memories of courtship, runaway slaves, abolitionist and suffragette movements, the popularity of seances, medical advances, and current inventions along with the issues of war and peace, freedom of religion, and the value of education.

Introducing the Book
This slim novel for high school students will have a special appeal to girls and can serve as a catalyst for further reading about events and issues presented in this book. Reading aloud the first chapter will help students past the flashback device used to begin the story. This is a perfect curriculum tie-in for an American history or issues class.

Booktalks

In the Aisle
There was a time when some houses had a special room to be born in, to be sick in, and to die in. Georgina tells her family's life story through the events that took place in their borning room. She speaks of the fear of hiding a runaway slave, being a child and helping to deliver a baby, and the new fascination with seances.

With the Author's Words

Just prior to the Civil War some slaves are struggling north toward freedom. Georgina and her family are abolitionists, even though they know there is a penalty for assisting and sheltering runaway slaves.

> *It was the next morning that I found the runaway. I was picking berries in the woods behind the pasture and throwing stones at tree trunks, wishing that I'd been born a boy, when I saw her on the ground. She was sprawled on her side. I was sure she was dead. My skin went icy, my stomach hot as lava. I dropped my pail—and she sprang up. "Lord!" she cried. "Spare old Cora!"* (P. 18, hardback edition)

What can Georgina do to help Cora without putting her own family in jeopardy? This is just one of the exciting events told by Georgina in *The Borning Room* by Paul Fleischman.

Literature Extensions/Alternative Book Report Activities

American History/Geography—The Underground Railroad is a significant theme in *The Borning Room*, and it continues to fascinate students. Provide a classroom library consisting of the books listed in the accompanying bookmark for further study.

A related video, *Underground Railroad: Escape to Freedom* (BackPax International) features runaway slave characters who describe their escapes. Jeanette Winter's *Follow the Drinking Gourd* (Alfred A. Knopf, 1988) is a picture book for all ages about the Underground Railroad. A video version is available from American School Publishers (1990).

Some of the routes and safehouses that escaping slaves used can be documented in surviving records. Charles Blockson's *The Underground Railroad* (Berkley, 1987) is a good resource. Also consult his article, "Escape From Slavery: The Underground Railroad" *National Geographic* 166(1): 3-39, July 1984. Another source is Glennete Turner's *Underground Railroad in DuPage County, Illinois* (Newman Educational, 1986). Turner recommends that students try to imagine what it was like to be an escaping slave.

American History/Issues—Important historical issues are dealt with in *The Borning Room*. Students can do detailed research specifically on the abolitionist movement, the Underground Railroad, secession of the Southern states, the Emancipation Proclamation, and the beliefs and actions of the Quakers. Those students interested in the suffragette movement could explore suffragette stands on education, the poor, and voting rights.

History/Folklore—Every culture's folklore is composed of customs, legends, beliefs, and superstitions. Certainly the characters in *The Borning Room* were influenced by their superstitious beliefs. They thought thunder meant someone was going to die, taking stoppers out of bottles would ease the pain of childbirth, that a bird in the house brings death, and so on. Whether or not these ideas are believable, most folklorists and anthropologists regard superstitions as imaginative expressions of a culture. Individual students or the class can do further research to uncover other fascinating bits of folklore. Consider comparing superstitions from different cultures.

Literature/Reading Aloud—Georgina's family spent their evenings listening to classical music and reading aloud to each other for enjoyment. This important activity no longer occurs in most families. However, everybody loves to be read to, and it is a valuable activity for young adults. Jim Trelease, the noted read-aloud specialist, says that reading aloud is an activity that takes place at both Cambridge and Oxford universities in England. He has said, "I get the distinct impression that if it's good enough for Oxford and Cambridge it's good enough for any elementary school, junior high or high school in the United States." Choose some literature to share aloud with your students and encourage them to read aloud excerpts from some of their favorite books.

Paul Fleischman Wrote:

The Animal Hedge

The Borning Room

Coming-and-Going Men

Finzel the Farsighted

Graven Images

I Am Phoenix: Poems for Two Voices

Joyful Noise: Poems for Two Voices

Path of the Pale Horse

Phoebe Danger, Detective in the Case of the Two-Minute Cough

Rondo in C

Saturnalia

Historical Novels of the 1800s

Blos, Joan W. *A Gathering of Days: A New England Girl's Journal, 1830-32*

Clapp, Patricia. *The Tamarack Tree*

Collier, James Lincoln, and Christopher Collier. *The Clock*

Fleischman, Paul. *The Borning Room*

Forman, James D. *Becca's Story*

Harder, Janet D. *Letters from Carrie*

Paterson, Katherine. *Lyddie*

Paulsen, Gary. *Nightjohn*

Rinaldi, Ann. *The Last Silk Dress*

———. *Wolf by the Ears*

Roberts, Willo Davis. *Jo and the Bandit*

Shore, Laura. *The Sacred Moon Tree*

Terris, Susan. *Nell's Quilt*

Wallace, Bill. *Buffalo Gal*

Wisler, G. Clifton. *Red Cap*

The Underground Railroad

Armstrong, Jennifer. *Steal Away*

Beatty, Patricia. *Jayhawker*

———. *Who Comes with Cannons?*

Blockson, Charles. *The Underground Railroad*

Blos, Joan W. *A Gathering of Days: A New England Girl's Journal, 1830-32*

Cosner, Shaaron. *The Underground Railroad*

Fleischman, Paul. *The Borning Room*

Hamilton, Virginia. *The House of Dies Drear*

Rappaport, Doreen. *Escape from Slavery: Five Journeys to Freedom*

Reiss, Kathryn. *Time Windows*

Smucker, Barbara. *Runaway to Freedom: A Story of the Underground Railway*

Winter, Jeanette. *Follow the Drinking Gourd*

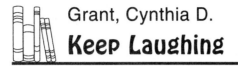

Grant, Cynthia D.
Keep Laughing

LC 91-6816, ©1991, 163p., $14.95 (ISBN 0-689-3154-7), Atheneum

Genre: Contemporary realistic fiction

Themes: Fathers and sons, comedians, love, abandonment, career versus family, decision making, celebrities, selfishness, driving, independence, school life, boy-girl relationships, anger, single-parent families

Reading level: Fifth grade

Interest level: Seventh through twelfth grades

Reviews:
Booklist. 88(5):506 November 1, 1991
School Library Journal. 37(9):278 September, 1991. (Starred)
Voice of Youth Advocates. 14(6):370 February, 1992. (#4 quality, #3 popularity)

Author Information

Cynthia D. Grant was born in Massachusetts and moved to California with her family when she was twelve. Compelled to write, she says she sometimes loves it and sometimes feels "like chucking my typewriter out the window." Grant considers herself a feminist and avoids stereotypes in her books. She says she prefers to make her points humorously, because readers are more receptive when they are being entertained. The first winner of the PEN/Norma Klein Award, Grant lives in the mountains near Cloverdale, California, with her husband and sons.

Plot Summary

Abandoned by his father and overloved and smothered by his mother, fifteen-year-old Shepherd Youngman tries to come to terms with his life. Shepherd enjoys attention when he smarts off in class, but his sadness is scarcely concealed. When his flamboyant father, a comedian, tries to make amends and reenter Shepherd's life, Shepherd eventually realizes the truth of his father's empty promises.

Introducing the Book

To introduce the book, read aloud the untitled preface. *Keep Laughing* was included on the 1992 ALA/YALSA Recommended Books for the Reluctant Young Adult Reader list.

Booktalks

In the Aisle

Most people probably think it's great to have a famous and funny dad. But Shepherd knows the truth. His dad has never been around much and now arrives expecting to be welcomed back by a grateful son. Would a convertible be enough to win your unquestioning love?

With the Author's Words

Having a famous and funny father seems terrific, but Shepherd knows the truth. His comedian father went away when he was a baby and hasn't been around much these past fifteen years. Shepherd knows comedy and tragedy.

> *People think comedians are naturally funny. Not true! A comedian is the saddest guy around! It's like hiring a pyromaniac to be the fire chief! Sure, he's an expert in his field, but is he the right man for the job?... I want to leave you with a thought: He who laughs, lasts, and he who cries, dies. So no matter what happens, keep laughing. Don't stop! No matter what happens, keep laughing.* (From the preface, hardback edition)

It's hard to *Keep Laughing* when you can't count on your dad.

Literature Extensions/Alternative Book Report Activities

Drama/Comedy Performances/Careers—Like Shepherd, students in your class may be naturally funny. Encourage them to develop an act and stage their own comedy club performances.

Some helpful books may be *Growing Up Laughing: Humorists Look at American Youth* edited by Charles Keller (Prentice-Hall, 1981), *Comic Lives: Inside the World of Stand-Up Comedy* by Betsy Borns (Simon & Schuster, 1987), and *So You Want to be a Star: A Teenager's Guide to Breaking into Show Business* by Randi Reisfeld (Pocket Books, 1990).

Contemporary Issues/Child Support—Shepherd and his mother have always had a difficult time financially because his dad was not consistent with child support payments. This issue is addressed by existing state laws that undergo constant revision. What are the current laws in your state? What enforcement procedure is in place? What steps have state and federal governments taken to help improve enforcement?

Helpful books include *The Practical Child Support Collection Workbook* by Gary L. Callahan (Charis, 1991), *The Teenage Parent's Child Support Guide* by Bary T. Schnell (Advocacy Center for Child Support, 1988), *Fathers' Rights: The Sourcebook for Understanding and Dealing with the Child Support System* by Jon Conine (Walker, 1989), and *Child Support: How to Get What Your Child Needs and Deserves* by Carole A. Chambers (Summit, 1991).

Creative Writing—Shepherd is not overly impressed with his fortune cookie message (P. 72, hardback edition). Have students take a chance and select a cookie with a message to use as a topic for an essay. Or as a class or individual project, students can compose their own topical and specific fortunes and make cookies for everyone!

Journalism/Interviews—Shepherd's father was interviewed by *People* magazine. Provide students with multiple copies of *People* as well as news journals (*Newsweek, Business Week, Time*, etc.). Students can compare and contrast interview styles. Interested students can interview someone of their choice and write their interviews in various styles.

School Daze

Avi. *Nothing but the Truth: A Documentary Novel*

Hopper, Nancy J. *The Interrupted Education of Huey B.*

Klass, David. *Wrestling with Honor*

Korman, Gordon. *Don't Care High*

———. *A Semester in the Life of a Garbage Bag*

Mayer, Barbara. *How to Succeed in High School*

Naylor, Phyllis Reynolds. *The Year of the Gopher*

Paulsen, Gary. *The Boy Who Owned the School*

Peck, Richard. *Princess Ashley*

Posner, Richard. *Goodnight, Cinderella*

Stone, Bruce. *Been Clever Forever*

Wolff, Virginia Euwer. *Probably Still Nick Swansen*

Wyss, Thelma. *Here at the Scenic-Vu Motel*

Zindel, Paul. *A Begonia for Miss Applebaum*

Car and Driver

Berger, K. T. *Zen Driving*

Donofrio, Beverly. *Riding in Cars with Boys: Confessions of a Bad Girl Who Made Good*

Hensel, George. *Learn to Drive*

Soor, Ron, and Nancy Soor. *In the Driver's Seat*

Sports Illustrated eds. *Sports Illustrated Safe Driving*

Stein, Wendy. *Taking the Wheel*

Stewart, Jackie, and Alan Henry. *Jackie Stewart's Principles of Performance Driving*

Thesman, Jean. *When Does the Fun Start?*

Laughing Out Loud!

Clarke, J. *The Heroic Life of Al Capsella*

Fine, Anne. *The Book of the Banshee*

Gale, David, ed. *Funny You Should Ask: The Delacorte Book of Original Humorous Short Stories*

Koertge, Ron. *Where the Kissing Never Stops*

Korman, Gordon. *Don't Care High*

Naylor, Phyllis Reynolds. *The Year of the Gopher*

Okimoto, Jean Davies. *Jason's Women*

Stone, Bruce. *Been Clever Forever*

Thompson, Julian. *Simon Pure*

Hobbs, Will
Downriver

LC 90-001044, ©1991, 204p., $13.95 (ISBN 0-689-31690-9), Atheneum. Paperback $3.50 (ISBN 0-553-29717-1), Bantam Books

Genres: Contemporary realistic fiction, adventure

Themes: Wilderness programs, cooperation, survival, friendship, choices, trust, love, whitewater rafting, running away, self-discovery, problem solving, family relationships, nature, Grand Canyon, camping

Reading level: Sixth grade

Interest level: Seventh through twelfth grades

Reviews:
Booklist. 87(13):1377 March 1, 1991
Bulletin of the Center for Children's Books. 44(7):7166-67 March, 1991. (Recommended)
School Library Journal. 37(3):212 March, 1991
Voice of Youth Advocates. 14(3):171-72 August, 1991. (#4 quality, #4 popularity)

Author Information
A teacher in the Durango, Colorado, public schools, Will Hobbs is a graduate of Stanford University. His home in Durango is near the Weminuche Wilderness, and he frequently goes backpacking with his family and friends.

Plot Summary
Fifteen-year-old Jessie has been sent to a wilderness therapy program along with three other girls and four boys. The rebellious eight refer to themselves as "Hoods in the Woods." They're supposed to be learning responsible decision-making skills and developing positive interpersonal relationships. When Troy, an influential member of the group, suggests they steal the van and run the forbidden Colorado River without adult supervision, the rest of them agree with alacrity. With luck and their new survival and cooperation skills, the group successfully navigates the early rapids. However, the eventual power struggles combined with the increasingly dangerous rapids cause the ultimate breakdown of the group.

Introducing the Book
Read aloud to the end of the first paragraph in chapter 2 (p. 11, hardback edition). This introduction quickly launches the reader into the wilderness setting and the group dynamics. Don't let the 204-page length deter potential readers. The quick pace and excitement will sustain even the most reluctant reader. Consider asking a river guide for the Colorado River through the Grand Canyon to assist in introducing the book. *Downriver* was included on the 1992 ALA/YALSA Recommended Books for the Reluctant Young Adult Reader list.

Booktalks

In the Aisle
The eight rebellious "Hoods in the Woods" are sure that they can make it on their own. But they don't know the power, the strength, and the danger that await them when they run away to raft the whitewater through the Grand Canyon. They expect huge rapids but are unprepared for freezing rain, injuries, and fighting among themselves. It is the ultimate challenge.

With the Author's Words
They are eight troubled teens sent to the wilderness to learn how to behave. They are on their way to raft the calm San Juan River when their adult supervisor leaves them alone in the van.

> *"So why don't we run the Grand Canyon?" There followed several moments of total silence, a rare event for the eight of us. It was an awesome thought, outrageous and inspired. There was a beauty to the idea, grand, wild, and majestic, drawing power and mystery from the canyon itself. You'd have to be awfully nervy to think you could up and run the Grand Canyon, as inexperienced as we were. No adults, just us.* (P. 51, hardback edition)

It's strictly against the rules—and not a safe time to run the Grand Canyon even with adults. What a great idea! Join them as they head *Downriver.*

Literature Extensions/Alternative Book Report Activities

Archaeology—The mountains throughout the Southwest have clues to past civilizations, such as the Anasazi cliff dwellers. National parks like Mesa Verde and Bandelier provide educational experiences through tours, museums, and marked trails. Throughout the United States, archaeological digs continue to uncover new information about past civilizations and cultures.

For interested students, provide materials and travel information for further research or reports. David Macaulay's *Motel of the Mysteries* (Houghton Mifflin, 1979) is a satire on archaeology and civilizations and can provide an excellent introduction to the study of archaeology.

Other books include *New Treasures of the Past* by Brian M. Fagan (Barron's Educational Series, 1987), *The Practical Archaeologist* by James McIntosh (Facts on File, 1988), *Mysteries of the Ancient Americas* by editors of *Reader's Digest* (Reader's Digest Press, 1986), *Stones, Bones, and Ancient Cities* by Lawrence H. Robbins (St. Martin's Press, 1990), *Doorways Through Time: The Romance of Archaeology* by Stephen Bertman (Jeremy P. Tarcher, 1986), and *Discover Archaeology: An Introduction to the Tools and Techniques of Archaeological Fieldwork* by George Edward Sullivan (Doubleday, 1980).

Geology—The Grand Canyon is a geologist's dream because of its record of the Earth's history. The layers of rock and rock formations continue to give information about the Earth's origins and continually changing surface.

For more information about the Grand Canyon, provide *Running Wild: Through the Grand Canyon on the Ancient Path* by John Annerino (Harbinger House, 1992), *Canyon* by Michael Patrick Ghiglieri (University of Arizona Press, 1992), *Corridors of Time: 1,700,000,000 Years of Earth at Grand Canyon* by Ron Redfern (Times Books, 1983), *Secrets in the Grand Canyon, Zion and Bryce Canyon National Parks* by Lorraine Salem Tuffs (National Photographic Collections, 1992), *River Runners of the Grand Canyon* by David Lavender (University of Arizona Press, 1985), one of the many editions of *Grand Canyon: The Story Behind the Scenery* by Merrill D. Beal (KC Publications), and *A Wilderness Called the Grand Canyon* by Stewart W. Aitchison (Voyageur Press, 1991).

Students can investigate the geologic history of their own surroundings by exploring caves, hiking, conferring with local geologists, and so on. General books on geology include *A Field Manual for the Amateur Geologist: Tools and Activities for Exploring Our Planet* by Alan M. Cvancara (Prentice-Hall, 1985), *Suburban Geology* by Richard Headstrom (Prentice-Hall, 1985), and *Rocks and Minerals* by Chris Pellant (Houghton Mifflin, 1992).

History/Grand Canyon—In 1869, Major John Wesley Powell became the first white man to run the Colorado River through the Grand Canyon. Since then it has become one of the most fascinating places to visit in the West. Interested students can learn more by writing to obtain information or reading more about it.

Consult *The Man Who Walked Through Time* by Colin Fletcher (Alfred A. Knopf, 1967), *John Wesley Powell and the Great Survey of the American West* by Ann Gaines (Chelsea House, 1992), or *The Exploration of the Colorado River and Its Canyons* by John Wesley Powell (Dover, 1961).

Provide videotapes such as *Bryce National Park; Zion National Park; North Rim of the Grand Canyon* (Finley Holiday Films, 1980), *Grand Canyon National Park* (Finley Holiday Films), or *Great Wonders of the World Video* with Doug Jones (1992).

Science/Bird Songs—Freddie, one of the travelers, knows quite a lot about bird identification and recognizes varieties of birds by listening to their songs. Take students on a bird identification field trip or provide materials for further investigation, or both.

Helpful books include *A Field Guide to the Birds* by Roger Tory Peterson (Houghton Mifflin, 1980), *Birds of North America* by Chandler S. Robbins et al. (Western, 1983), and *Field Guide to the Birds of North America* by Shirley L. Scott (National Geographic Society, 1983). The National Geographic Society's *The Wonder of Birds* (1983) is a guide to 800 species of North American birds and also comes with a recording of bird sounds. Audiocassettes of bird songs are also available from other organizations.

Runaways

Calvert, Patricia. *When Morning Comes*

Hobbs, Will. *Bearstone*

———. *Downriver*

Jaspersohn, William. *Grounded*

Jones, Adrienne. *Street Family*

Kingsolver, Barbara. *The Bean Trees*

Major, Kevin. *Hold Fast*

Miller-Cachmann, Lyn. *Hiding Places*

Samuels, Gertrude. *Run, Shelley, Run*

Spinelli, Jerry. *Maniac Magee*

Wilderness Adventures

Carrier, Jim. *Down the Colorado: Travels in a Western Waterway*

Finkelstein, Dave, and Jack London. *Greater Nowheres: A Journey Through the Australian Bush*

Hauser, Hillary. *Call to Adventure*

Hildebrand, John. *Reading the River: A Voyage Down the Yukon*

LaBastile, Anne. *Women and Wilderness*

———. *Woodswoman*

Simpson, Joe. *Touching the Void*

Swendsen, David H. *Badge in the Wilderness: My 30 Dangerous Years Combating Wildlife Violators*

Survival Stories

Bauer, Marion Dane. *Face to Face*

Bell, William. *Crabb's Journey*

Blackwood, Gary. *Wild Timothy*

Eisenstadt, Jill. *From Rockaway*

Hobbs, Will. *Bearstone*

———. *Downriver*

Major, Kevin. *Hold Fast*

Paulsen, Gary. *Hatchet*

———. *The River*

Stevermer, Carolyn. *River Rats*

Thompson, Julian F. *Gypsyworld*

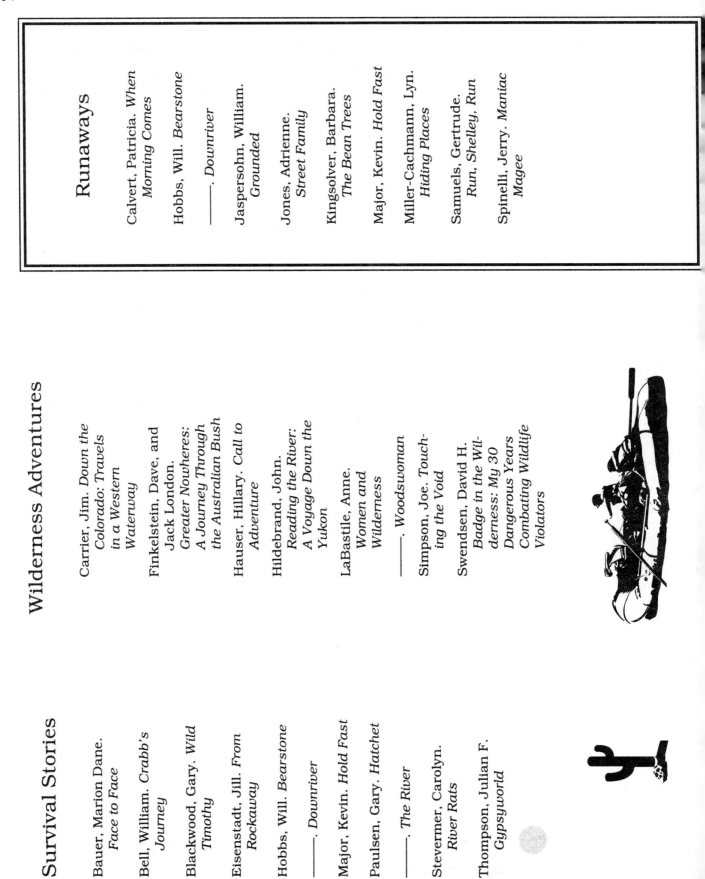

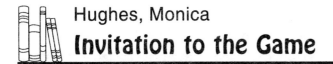

Hughes, Monica
Invitation to the Game

LC 90-22832, ©1990, 183p., $14.00 (ISBN 0-671-74236-1), Simon & Schuster

Genre: Science fiction

Themes: Cooperation, individuality, friendship, creativity, survival, freedom, pollution, space colonization, government, gangs, games, risks, robotics, unemployment, careers, overpopulation, artificial reality

Reading level: Sixth grade

Interest level: Seventh through twelfth grades

Reviews:
Booklist. 88(2):141 September 15, 1991
Bulletin of the Center for Children's Books. 45(2):40 October, 1991. (Recommended)
School Library Journal. 37(9):281 September, 1991. (Starred)
Voice of Youth Advocates. 14(5):323 December, 1991. (#2 quality, #2 popularity)

Author Information

Born in England in 1925, Monica Hughes has lived in several countries, including Egypt, Scotland, and Zimbabwe. As a child she discovered that she loved Jules Verne books. Hughes finally settled in Alberta, Canada, and has been writing since 1975. One of Canada's finest writers of science fiction for young people, Hughes was awarded the Canadian Vicky Metcalf Award for her work in 1981. Science fiction is her first love. She says, "I like to explore the feelings, the needs and ideals of young people in the world of tomorrow, hopefully bringing a universality to the specific." Hughes says that the primary function of a writer is to help children "explore the world and the future." She believes there must always be hope.

Plot Summary

The year is 2154 and the newest graduates of a Government School face either satisfying careers or lifelong unemployment. Job scarcity has resulted from the widespread use of robots in nearly every occupation. Lisse and five talented friends are dismayed to find themselves among the unemployed. In order to survive in a dangerous city, the friends band together and create a home in an abandoned warehouse. When they receive an invitation to "The Game," they are eager to participate but wonder why they are selected to play and whether "The Game" is real or an interactive fantasy (artificial reality). "The Game" becomes the focus of their communal existence as they work to improve their survival skills. The ultimate challenge is when they are left to survive on an alien planet.

Introducing the Book

The futuristic action of this book begins on the last day of boarding school (high school graduation). Although the story is narrated in the first person by Lisse, the gender representation throughout the book is equal, making this an action-packed winner for young adults of either gender. To hook potential readers, read aloud to page 10 (hardback edition) to "Or would some of my friends be there too?"

Booktalks

In the Aisle

Lisse and her friends have just graduated from their government school in the year 2154. They are astonished to learn they will join the masses of unemployed who live in restricted areas of dangerous, crime-ridden cities. The future looks bleak until they receive the highly coveted *Invitation to the Game*. Does this mean only temporary relief from their dreary lives or is there hope for their future?

With the Author's Words

The year is 2154 and six recent graduates of a government high school have been invited to play "The Game." They hope it will provide relief from the tensions of living in a dark and dangerous world filled with gangs, thought police, high unemployment, and intense government control. During "The Game," they find themselves transported to an unknown location. In the midst of scaling a rock cliff, Lisse has the most trouble keeping up.

> *I'd almost reached the bottom when my fingers finally let me down and I swung outward. I had time to scream a warning, so that those below me could get out of the way, and to think: I'm going to land on my back on the rocks and my spine will be broken. What a stupid waste! There was no pain. Only a whirling sensation and blackness.* (P. 69, hardback edition)

Is this Game real or are the experiences induced by computer and video simulation? What happens when Lisse wakes up? Consider this your *Invitation to the Game.*

Literature Extensions/Alternative Book Report Activities

Sociology/Utopian Society—Lisse and her seven friends have to develop a new society on an alien planet They are eager not to make the same mistakes that destroyed the planet Earth. Carefully they plan their new society, guarding against pollution and wisely using their resources (see p. 162+, hardback edition). Students can design a utopian society, describing it by essay writing, by creating an architectural model, or by writing a futuristic science fiction story.

Sociology/Group Dynamics/Gangs—This book looks at both the positive and the negative aspects of group dynamics. Lisse's group works for positive change, while the violent marauding gangs of the streets are destructive. The proliferation of gangs and gang-related problems in our society is well documented. Students can learn more about gang activity by researching articles in current periodicals and newspapers. An example is "No Way Out" by Jon D. Hull, *Time* 140(7): 38-40, August 17, 1992.

Are there gangs in your community? What part do gangs play in crime, drug use, violence, destruction of property, and so on? What opportunities are offered to include gang members in productive community activities? Use the compiled information to stage a debate, write a newspaper article, role play, interview a gang member, and so forth.

Useful books include *People and Folks: Gangs, Crime and the Underclass in a Rustbelt City* by John Hagedorn (Lake View Press, 1988), *Out of the Gang* by Keith Elliott Greenberg (Lerner, 1992), *Street Gangs in America* by Sandra Gardner (Franklin Watts, 1992), *Street Gangs: Gaining Turf, Losing Ground* by Roger Rosen and Patra McSharry (Rosen, 1991), and *Coping with Street Gangs* by Margot Webb (Rosen, 1990).

Science/Folk Medicine—Lisse and her friends are new inhabitants of an alien planet and must do without modern medical equipment and supplies. Certain group members have a scientific understanding of the medicinal properties of particular plants. Many students will be interested in investigating the historically documented healing effects certain plants have.

Make the following reference books available for further information: *Folklore on the American Land* by Duncan Emrich (Little, Brown, 1972), *Rodale's Illustrated Encyclopedia of Herbs* by Claire Kowalchik and William H. Hylton (Rodale Press, 1987), *Guide to Plants and Flowers* by Francesco Bianchini and Azzurra Carrasa Pantano (Simon & Schuster, 1989), *Folk Medicine* by Marc Kusinitz (Chelsea House, 1991), and *Chinese Herbal Medicine* by Daniel P. Reid (Shambhala Publications, 1992).

Science/Robotics—Many jobs in the futuristic *Invitation to the Game* are accomplished by robots who replace humans. Students can research the extent to which robots are currently used. If possible, invite someone in your area who has developed a robot to demonstrate its use at your school. Encourage students to build their own robots and provide books like the following: *Build Your Own Working Robot: The Second Generation* by David L. Heiserman (TAB Books, 1987) and *The Robot Builder's Bonanza: 99 Inexpensive Robotics Projects* by Gordon McComb (TAB Books, 1987).

For further research into the increasing use of robots, students can refer to *Robots: Your High-Tech World* by Gloria Skurzynski (Bradbury Press, 1991), *Mind Children: The Future of Robot and Human Intelligence* by Hans Moravec (Harvard University Press, 1988), *The Omni Book of Computers and Robots* by Owen Davies (Zebra, 1983), *Radical Robots: Can You Be Replaced?* by George Harrar and Linda Harrar (Simon & Schuster, 1990), and *Robots, Machines in Man's Image* by Isaac Asimov and Karen A. Frenkel (Robotic Industries, 1985).

Monica Hughes Wrote:

Beyond the Dark River

Devil on My Back

The Dream Catcher

The Guardian of Isis

Hunter in the Dark

Invitation to the Game

The Isis Pedlar

Keeper of the Isis Light

The Promise

Ring-Rise, Ring-Set

Playing in the Future— Sci Fi

Baird, Thomas. *Smart Rats*

Banks, Ian M. *The Player of Games*

Card, Orson Scott. *Ender's Game*

Chetwin, Grace. *Out of the Dark World*

Hughes, Monica. *Invitation to the Game*

Longyear, Barry B. *Sea of Glass*

Orwell, George. *1984*

Rubenstein, Gillian. *Skymaze*

——. *Space Demons*

Velde, Vivian Vande. *User Friendly*

Gangs

Bunting, Eve. *Jumping the Nail*

Cross, Gillian. *A Map of Nowhere*

Forshay-Lunsford, Cin. *Walk Through Cold Fire*

French, Michael. *Us Against Them*

Hinton, S. E. *The Outsiders*

——. *Rumble Fish*

——. *That Was Then, This Is Now*

Hoffman, Alice. *Property Of*

Hughes, Monica. *Invitation to the Game*

Katz, Steve. *Florry of Washington Heights*

L'Engle, Madeleine. *The Young Unicorns*

Myers, Walter Dean. *Scorpions*

Peck, Richard. *Secrets of a Shopping Mall*

Thompson, Julian F. *Gypsyworld*

Klause, Annette Curtis
The Silver Kiss

LC 89-48880, 198p., ©1990, $14.95 (ISBN 0-385-30160-X), Delacorte Press. Paperback $3.50 (ISBN 0-440-21346-0), Dell

---

Genres: Fantasy, contemporary realistic fiction

Themes: Vampires, friendship, death, loneliness, revenge, mortality, good versus evil, romance, love, truth, cancer, guilt, compassion

Reading level: Sixth grade

Interest level: Seventh through twelfth grades

Reviews:
Booklist. 87(4):439 October 15, 1990. (Starred)
School Library Journal. 36(9):255 September, 1990. (Starred)
Voice of Youth Advocates. 13(5):299 December, 1990. (#4 quality, #4 popularity)

Author Information
Annette Curtis Klause grew up in England and was read to and sung to a lot as a child. She began writing early, producing poetry, plays, and what she calls, a "gruesome story" titled "The Blood Ridden Pool of Solen Goom." Seeds of inspiration for *The Silver Kiss* came from the first vampire book she read, *The Shiny Narrow Grin* by Jane Gaskill. Klause moved to the United States at age fifteen. About the character Simon in *The Silver Kiss* Klause says, "There's a lot of my past in him—both the yearning for affection, and the underlying anger and violence." Klaus, a children's librarian in Maryland, has written several articles for children's literature magazines and reviews books for *School Library Journal*. *The Silver Kiss* is her first novel.

Plot Summary
Zoë's world is falling apart. Her mother is dying from cancer, her father is distracted and distraught, and her best friend is moving away. Befriended by the strange and intriguing Simon, Zoë becomes close to him despite a feeling of discomfort. When Simon trusts her enough to reveal his true vampire self, Zoë becomes caught up in his plan to destroy his evil vampire brother. Because of Simon's vast experience with death and his wish to end his own "life," he is able to offer Zoë compassion in dealing with the imminent death of her mother.

Introducing the Book
Romance and vampires—it doesn't get much better than this! If you need to sell this title, read aloud the first two chapters (one in Zoë's voice and one in Simon's) to page 19 and be prepared with multiple copies. *The Silver Kiss* was included on the 1991 ALA/YALSA Recommended Books for the Reluctant Young Adult Reader list.

Booktalks

In the Aisle
Life can't get much worse for Zoë. Her mother is dying, her father is distraught and can't help her, and her best friend is moving away. And then Simon shows up. Is he somehow connected to the murders happening in her town? He is strangely appealing but also seems potentially dangerous.

With the Author's Words

Zoë needed some time to herself and walked in the park late at night, in spite of the recent murders in her town.

> *Moonlight lit the gazebo, tracing it with silver, but a shadow crept inside, independent of natural shades. She tensed. Her hands gripped the edge of the bench.... She saw someone within. A figure detached from the shadows. Her mouth dried. Mother of two found dead, she thought. It moved toward her, stepped into the moonlight on the side closest to her, and briefly she thought to run. Then she saw his face.* (Pp. 11-12, hardback edition)

This face stops Zoë's flight. Why? What is it about this boy, and what is his connection to *The Silver Kiss*?

Literature Extensions/Alternative Book Report Activities

Communication/Counseling—Zoë's family is unable to cope with her mother's illness and impending death. This is a typical response, because many people know little about dealing with these issues. Invite a counselor or hospice member to lead a discussion about death and dying.

Provide some of the many resources available to teach coping skills for similar situations. These include *I Don't Know What to Say: How to Help and Support Someone Who Is Dying* by Robert Buckman (Key Port Books, 1988), Elisabeth Kubler-Ross's *Living with Death and Dying* (Macmillan, 1981), *To Live Until We Say Good-bye* (Prentice, 1978), by Elisabeth Kubler-Ross and M. Warshaw, *The Hospice Alternative: A New Context for Death and Dying* by Anne Munley (Basic Books, 1983), *Gentle Closings: How to Say Good-bye to Someone You Love* by Ted Menten (Running Press, 1992), *Teenagers Face to Face with Bereavement* by Karen Gravelle and Charles Haskins (Messner, 1989), and *Letting Go with Love: The Grieving Process* by Nancy O'Connor (La Mariposa, 1985).

Creative Writing—Zoë is a poet and she writes to help herself deal with personal problems. She writes a poem titled "Spells Against Death" (Pp. 75 and 145, hardback edition) and slips it beneath her dying mother's hand. The reader never sees the actual poem, but interested students can write their own "Spells Against Death."

Folklore—Vampire mythology is present in many cultures. Simon mentions traveling with earth from his homeland, the destructive power of sunlight, and the stake-through-the-heart method of killing a vampire—all familiar elements connected with vampire lore.

Refer interested students to other materials on this subject such as *The Dracula Scrapbook: Articles, Essays, Letters, Newspaper Cuttings, Anecdotes, Illustrations, Photographs and Memorabilia About the Vampire Legend* edited by Peter Haining (Bramhall House, 1976).

Literature/Media—For generations, stories about Dracula and other vampires have appeared in various media. Provide Bram Stoker's original *Dracula*, using the edition illustrated by Greg Hildebrandt (Unicorn, 1985), as well as *Hollywood Gothic: The Tangled Web of Dracula from Novel to Stage to Screen* by David J. Skal (W. W. Norton, 1990), *Blood Is Not Enough: Seventeen Stories of Vampires* by Edward Bryant, *The Penguin Book of Vampire Stories* (Penguin Books, 1987), compiled by Alan Ryan, and *Vampires: A Collection of Original Stories* edited by Jane Yolen and Martin H. Greenberg (HarperCollins, 1991).

Death

Allen, R. E. *Ozzy on the Outside*

Carter, Alden R. *Wart, Son of Toad*

Grant, Cynthia D. *Phoenix Rising: Or, How to Survive Your Life*

Klause, Annette Curtis. *The Silver Kiss*

Naylor, Phyllis Reynolds. *The Dark of the Tunnel*

Schwandt, Stephen. *Holding Steady*

Stretton, Barbara. *You Never Lose*

Love Stories

Allman, Paul. *The Knot*

Bennett, Jay. *I Never Said I Loved You*

Callan, Jamie. *Just Too Cool*

Davis, Jenny. *Sex Education*

Davis, Leila. *Lover Boy*

Klause, Annette Curtis. *The Silver Kiss*

Klein, Norma. *Just Friends*

Mahy, Margaret. *The Changeover: A Supernatural Romance*

Nathan, Robert. *Portrait of Jennie*

Quin-Harkin, Janet. *Summer Heat*

Tyler, Vicky. *Danny and the Real Me*

Vampires

Aldiss, Brian W. *Dracula Unbound*

Cooney, Caroline B. *The Return of the Vampire*

Cusick, Richie Tankersley. *Vampire*

Fenn, Lionel. *The Mark of the Moderately Vicious Vampire*

Garden, Nancy. *My Sister, the Vampire*

Golden, Christie. *Vampire of the Mists*

Klause, Annette Curtis. *The Silver Kiss*

Pierce, Meredith. *The Darkangel Trilogy*

Plante, Edmund. *Alone in the House*

Saberhagen, Fred. *The Dracula series*

Scott, R. C. *Blood Sport*

Smith, L. J. *The Vampire Diaries series*

Steakley, John. *Vampire$*

Yarbro, Chelsea Quinn. *The Saint-Germain Chronicles*

Koertge, Ron
The Boy in the Moon

LC 89-15398, ©1990, 166p., $14.95 (ISBN 0-316-50102-6), Little, Brown. Paperback $3.99 (ISBN 0-380-71474-4), AvonFlare

Genres: Contemporary realistic fiction, humor

Themes: Coming of age, friendship, self-esteem, self-acceptance, family life, romance, boy-girl relationships, school life, alcoholism, sex, poetry, divorce, religion, acne

Reading level: Seventh grade

Interest level: Ninth through twelfth grades

Reviews:
Booklist. 86(13):1276 March 1, 1990
Bulletin of the Center for Children's Books.
  43(10):243-44 June, 1990. (Recommended)
Horn Book. 66(4):462 July/August, 1990
School Library Journal. 36(5):122 May, 1990
Voice of Youth Advocates. 13(3):160 August, 1990

Author Information

Ron Koertge (pronounced Kur-chee) was born in Illinois. He graduated from the University of Illinois and the University of Arizona. A writer of poetry and novels, Koertge is a professor of English at Pasadena City College in California. His first two young adult books began as failed adult novels. Koertge says his books are funny and appeal to teen readers because he has "a peculiar sense of humor." Considered an activist because he writes frankly about teenagers and sexual issues, Koertge says expounding on these themes is inevitable. So far Koertge has come up with an idea each year for a new book, but he worries about what will happen when that stops.

Plot Summary

The senior year of three best friends, Kevin, Nick, and Frieda, is fraught with change and their impending separation when they graduate. Kevin returns from a California summer and seems superficial and changed by his glamorous experiences. Meanwhile, Nick and Frieda's platonic relationship has moved to another level. Kevin's problems with an alcoholic father and needy younger brother draw the threesome together as they mature and develop.

Introducing the Book

Themes of first love, humor, and friendship along with an honest handling of sensitive issues create a must-read for both boys and girls. However, the frank language and intimate situations make this better for personal reading. Read aloud to the middle of page 15 ("Kevin?") to entice potential readers. The appeal of this book lies in the combination of themes and the humor. Though the hardcover jacket art is unappealing, the paperback art is quite attractive.

Booktalks

In the Aisle

Don't let the strange hardback cover dissuade you from reading Nick's hilarious story of his senior year. Nick's acne problem turns out to be the least of his worries. Best friend Kevin needs his help to save his younger brother from his alcoholic father. And Nick's feelings for his other best friend, Frieda, are suddenly changing.

With the Author's Words

When Kevin returns from his summer in California, he can't stop comparing dreary old Missouri to glamorous California. The first day back at school he and his two best friends, Frieda and Nick, are talking when Kevin remarks:

> *"Poor Sherry has some hair in her nose. I couldn't help but see it. I mean, she was standing right over me and...."*
> *"Kevin, everybody's got hair in their nose."*
> *"Not in L.A. Everything's clean as a whistle out there. The girls are perfect. Under their arms. Their legs. Everything flawless."*
> *"Compared to the enormously hairy Midwest?"*
> *"I'll see you guys later," said Frieda. "I'm going home and shave my entire body inside and out."* (P. 32, hardback edition)

Kevin's funny facade hides the serious problems he has to face now that he's home. Fortunately, he has best friends. He'll need them. *The Boy in the Moon*, otherwise known as Nick, is just one of those friends.

Literature Extensions/Alternative Book Report Activities

Creative Writing/Poetry—Nick's mother is an excellent poet and he often accompanies her to readings. Students in your class or school can stage a night when students read their original poetry.

English/Essays—The English senior project in Nick's class is to write an essay titled "WHO AM I?" His teacher insists that the opening sentence be dynamite, grasping the reader and not letting go until the end (Pp. 34-36, hardback edition). Students in your class can complete this assignment too with the same simple requirement: Length of the project is not important; the focus should be the honesty and power of the content.

Health/Skin Care—Nick is nearly obsessive about his acne. Like many teens, he tries every known cure. Provide students with materials about skin care such as pamphlets from health departments or physicians specializing in adolescent skin care. Some helpful books include *The Skin Doctor's Skin Doctoring Book* by Thomas Goodman (Sterling, 1984), *Skin and Its Care* by Brian Ward (Franklin Watts, 1990), and *Super Skin: A Leading Dermatologist's Guide to the Latest Breakthroughs in Skin Care* by Nelson Lee Novick (Crown, 1988).

Physical Education/Fitness—Nick's father is in wonderful physical condition and enjoys every minute of exercising. Kevin returns from California with a changed body after spending the summer working out on a Nautilus machine. Does your school's physical education curriculum focus on developing interest in lifetime sports? If not, consider exposing students to sports activities that can be enjoyed throughout their lives.

Helpful books include *Awesome Teen: Smart Choices for the 90s* by Chris Silkwood and Nancy Levicky (MasterMedia, 1991) and *Good Sports: Plain Talk About Health and Fitness for Teens* by Nissa Simon (Thomas Y. Crowell, 1990). A related video is *Teen Workout* (Random House Home Video, 1990).

Fathers and Sons

Carter, Alden R. *Wart, Son of Toad*

Christian, Mary Blount. *Linc*

Close, Jessie. *The Warping of Al*

Crutcher, Chris. *Athletic Shorts*

Grant, Cynthia. *Keep Laughing*

Koertge, Ron. *The Boy in the Moon*

———. *Mariposa Blues*

Peck, Richard. *Father Figure*

Salassi, Otto. *On the Ropes*

Stone, Bruce. *Half Nelson, Full Nelson*

Van Raven, Pieter. *A Time of Troubles*

Voigt, Cynthia. *Solitary Blue*

Girls to Women— Growing Up

Casely, Judith. *Kisses*

Forshay-Lunsford, Cin. *Walk Through Cold Fire*

Mazer, Norma Fox, and Harry Mazer. *Heartbeat*

Plummer, Louise. *My Name Is Sus5an Smith. The 5 Is Silent*

Schieber, Phyllis. *Strictly Personal*

Wersba, Barbara. *The Farewell Kid*

Zindel, Paul. *The Girl Who Wanted a Boy*

Boys to Men— Growing Up

Bunn, Scott. *Just Hold On*

Clarke, J. *The Heroic Life of Al Capsella*

Clements, Bruce. *Tom Loves Anna Loves Tom*

Ferris, Jean. *Across the Grain*

Frank, Elizabeth Bales. *Cooder Cutlas*

Koertge, Ron. *The Boy in the Moon*

Matthews, Greg. *Little Red Rooster*

Sommers, Beverly. *What Do Girls Want?*

Strasser, Todd. *A Very Touchy Subject*

Kuklin, Susan

What Do I Do Now?
Talking About Teenage Pregnancy

LC 90-45775, ©1991, 179p., $15.95 (ISBN 0-399-21843-2), Putnam. Paperback $7.95 (ISBN 0-399-22043-7), Putnam Publishing Group

Genre: Nonfiction

Themes: Teen pregnancy, sex education, prenatal care, decisions, health, birth control, Planned Parenthood, adoption, abortion, teen marriage, counseling, child care

Reading level: Sixth grade

Interest level: Seventh through twelfth grades

Reviews:
Booklist. 87(20):1952 June 15, 1991
Bulletin of the Center for Children's Books. 45(3):66-67 November, 1991. (Recommended and starred)
School Library Journal. 37(7):94-95 July, 1991. (Starred)
Voice of Youth Advocates. 14(3):190 August, 1991. (#5 quality, #4 popularity)

Author Information

A library lover in her childhood, Susan Kuklin graduated from New York University with a major in theater. She has been an English teacher, film studies teacher, and curriculum developer. Her theater background enabled her to easily grasp the fundamentals of photography, and her career as a photographer began with a project for Planned Parenthood in the Appalachians. Kuklin worked as a photographer for five major magazines but was interested in looking at subjects in more detail. Thus began her writing and publishing career. Kuklin has a strong interest in social and humanitarian issues.

Plot Summary

Using first-person accounts of unplanned pregnancies, Kuklin quotes pregnant teenagers, their boyfriends, counselors, and medical personnel to present a realistic, firsthand look at this difficult situation. In a straightforward, nonjudgmental manner she writes about the hard choices and challenges facing pregnant teens—abortion, adoption, or keeping one's child. All of the teenagers interviewed were from the New York area but represent various age groups and ethnic and socioeconomic backgrounds. Glossary included.

Introducing the Book

Tell readers to skip the introduction and start with chapter 1, "Lynn and Drew." The book deals with personal and sensitive issues, so sharing this aloud is inappropriate. Many teens will be interested in reading this, so make it available—don't bury it in the nonfiction section! Display with other topical young adult materials and include it on book lists. This title appeared on the 1992 ALA/YALSA Recommended Books for the Reluctant Young Adult Reader list.

Booktalks

In the Aisle

Most teens don't have time for babies and have no idea how much work it is to be a parent. The teenagers in this book make difficult choices about their futures. Listen to these teen voices as they describe their situations and their lives in *What Do I Do Now?*

With the Author's Words

> "A few years ago my father said, 'If you ever come home pregnant, you might as well find some other place to live. You won't be living here.' So I thought, 'Well, I better not come home pregnant.'" (P. 29, hardback edition)

These are the words of sixteen-year-old Irene, whose pregnancy test came back negative. Many teens aren't that lucky and are left with the question: *What Do I Do Now?* Read Kuklin's book, which talks frankly about teenage pregnancy.

Literature Extensions/Alternative Book Report Activities

Debate/Research—Stage a debate on the abortion issue. Classic debate requires students to prepare arguments on both sides of the issue. Have your students research both the pro-life and pro-choice positions and be prepared to argue either side regardless of their personal beliefs. Challenge students to prepare their arguments so effectively that their listening peers are unsure of their actual beliefs. A book providing information on both sides of the issue is *The Abortion Controversy* by Carol Emmens (Messner, 1991).

Government/Demonstrations—Chapter 9 describes a pro-life demonstration occurring outside a health clinic. Throughout history demonstrations have been a powerful tool used to challenge policies or governments or both. Individuals or groups of students can focus on notable demonstrations (e.g., Martin Luther King, Jr.'s peace marches, antiwar demonstrations during the Vietnam War, the suffragette movement, the anti-apartheid movement, and the Red Square demonstrations in Moscow triggering the collapse of the Soviet Union). Individual or group presentations on these topics will illustrate the power of the people.

Health/Science/Math-Statistics—Look at the history, development, and effectiveness of all types of birth control, from rhythm through Norplant and the French abortion pill, RU486. Using statistics, evaluate the effectiveness of each birth control method.

Journalism—What help is available for unplanned pregnancies in your town, city, and state? Discover what options are accessible—abortion, adoption, help for teens who keep their babies, and so on. By contacting officials and agencies, students can research this issue and write a news story for publication in their school newspaper. If services are lacking, perhaps writing a letter to the community newspaper will focus attention on teen needs.

A useful reference tool is *Preventing Pregnancy, Protecting Health: A New Look at Birth Control Choices in the U.S.* by Susan Harlap et al. (Alan Guttmacher Institute, 1991).

Topical Books About Teen Issues

Arthur, Shirley. *Surviving Teen Pregnancy: Your Choices, Dreams, and Decisions*

Fleming, Alice. *What, Me Worry? How to Hang in When Your Problems Stress You Out*

Gilbert, Sara. *Get Help: Solving the Problems in Your Life*

Johnson, Eric W. *Love & Sex & Growing Up*

Keltner, Nancy, ed. *If You Print This, Please Don't Use My Name: Questions from Teens and Their Parents About Things That Matter*

Kuklin, Susan. *What Do I Do Now? Talking About Teenage Pregnancy*

Maloney, Michael, and Rachel Kranz. *Straight Talk About Anxiety and Depression*

McCoy, Kathy, and Charles Wibbelsman. *The New Teenage Body Book*

Newman, Susan. *Don't Be S.A.D.: A Teenage Guide to Handling Stress, Anxiety & Depression*

So Now You're a Parent

Baldwin, Rahima. *You Are Your Child's First Teacher*

Beyer, Kay. *Coping with Teen Parenting*

Bole, Janet. *Kids Still Having Kids: People Talk About Teen Pregnancy*

Franck, Irene, and David Brownstone. *The Parent's Desk Reference: The Ultimate Family Encyclopedia from Conception to College*

Gay, Kathlyn. *Daycare: Looking for Answers*

Gravelle, Karen, and Leslie Peterson. *Teenage Fathers*

Lindsay, Jeanne Warren, and Jean Brunelli. *Teens Parenting—Your Pregnancy and Newborn Journey: How to Take Care of Yourself and Your Newborn If You're a Pregnant Teen*

Paris, Thomas, and Eileen Paris. *"I'll Never Do to My Kids What My Parents Did to Me!" A Guide to Conscious Parenting*

Sanger, Singay, M.D. *Baby Talk/Parent Talk: Understanding Your Baby's Body Language*

Novels About Teen Pregnancy

Betancourt, Jeanne. *Sweet Sixteen and Never*

Calvert, Patrice. *Stranger, You & I*

Crompton, Anne Eliot. *Queen of Swords*

Doherty, Berlie. *Dear Nobody*

Eyerly, Jeanette. *Someone to Love Me*

Head, Ann. *Mr. and Mrs. Bo Jo Jones*

Klein, Norma. *No More Saturday Nights*

Kurland, Morton. *Our Sacred Honor*

Sandlin, Tim. *Skipped Parts*

Woodson, Jacqueline. *The Dear One*

Wurmfeld, Hope Herman. *Baby Blues*

Zindel, Paul. *My Darling, My Hamburger*

Lipsyte, Robert
The Brave

LC 90-25396, ©1991, 195p., $14.95 (ISBN 0-06-023915-8; ISBN 0-06-023916-6, library binding), HarperCollins

Genres: Contemporary realistic fiction, sports, multicultural

Themes: Self-discovery, friendship, acceptance, boxing, prison life, racism, street life, discipline, American Indians-Moscondaga, drug running, respect for nature

Reading level: Fifth grade

Reviews:
Booklist. 88(4):429 October 15, 1991
Bulletin of the Center for Children's Books. 45(3):68 November, 1991. (Recommended)
School Library Journal. 37(10):146 October, 1991. (Starred)
Voice of Youth Advocates. 14(5):314 December, 1991. (#5 quality, #5 popularity)

Interest level: Seventh through twelfth grades

Author Information

Robert Lipsyte is a journalist and television sports and news writer, in addition to being a writer of novels, biographies, and books about sports. As a child in New York City, Lipsyte was overweight and self-conscious, preferring to spend his time reading. He says he had the perfect childhood for a writer! After graduating from Columbia University at age nineteen, Lipsyte began his career at *The New York Times* as a copy boy and worked his way up to sports columnist. He says he became enamored with "the thunderous roar of the presses," and it was fourteen years before he quit *The Times* to devote himself to writing novels and screenplays. Lipsyte has been a sports essayist for "CBS News" and a correspondent specializing in sports for "NBC News." Drawing heavily on his experiences as a boxing reporter to write *The Contender*, Lipsyte believes strongly in having his books portray athletes who have ordinary problems in their lives. The idea for *The Brave* came from a journalism assignment at an American Indian reservation. Lipsyte met a young man who was afraid to stay and also afraid to leave. This youth did run away to New York, and his personal story of bravery and self-triumph impressed Lipsyte.

Plot Summary

Seventeen-year-old Sonny Bear is a boxer who has left the reservation to go to New York City. Immediately he is innocently sucked into an underground drug-running gang. Police Sergeant Albert Brooks attempts to save Sonny from a life of crime and imprisonment by guiding him to professional boxing training. Sonny's great-uncle, Jake, reminds Sonny how to incorporate the potential strength of his Moscondaga heritage. This is a sequel to Lipsyte's *The Contender* (HarperCollins, 1967). *The Chief* (HarperCollins, 1993) is the third book in The Contender series. *The Brave* was included on the 1992 ALA/YALSA Recommended Books for the Reluctant Young Adult Reader list.

Introducing the Book

To introduce the book, read the first two paragraphs or the first five paragraphs, or read to the bottom of page 12 (hardback edition). All three choices have great stopping points. The reading level is low, and the subject matter captivating and exciting. See *Book Links* 2(2): 38-40, November 1992, for more book connection strategies on *The Contender* and *The Brave*.

Booktalks

In the Aisle

Sonny Bear, *The Brave*, first meets Glen Hofer in a hillbilly boxing match. And so the story begins. They meet again in a big city bout at the book's end. What happens in between is for you to discover.

With the Author's Words

Upon his arrival at a city bus station, seventeen-year-old Sonny Bear unknowingly became involved in a drug ring. He was just talking to his "new friends" when suddenly their table was surrounded by half a dozen men.

> *"Okay, young gentlemen, that's enough, it's over." Hands on his shoulders. He glimpsed a dark face behind him. Sonny pivoted and nailed it with a left, a short crisp hook to the side of a bearded black chin. As the man crumpled, Sonny saw the badge hanging on a chain around his neck. A cop!* (P. 30, hardback edition)

Welcome to New York City, Sonny. How brave must you be?

Literature Extensions/Alternative Book Report Activities

Government/Prison System—Sonny finds out the hard way just how tough life can be in jail. Even though his crime is relatively minor, he finds himself incarcerated with hardened criminals. Teenagers can find out about the judicial system in their community and state. What facilities are available? Where are youths sent? What are the conditions? Tour such a facility, if possible. Does rehabilitation include increasing job skills and education? Are peer juries used?

A helpful book is *Think About Prisons and the Criminal Justice System* by Lois Smith Owens and Vivian Verdell Gordon (Walker, 1991).

Health/Drugs—The price was right for Sonny to agree to act as a courier for a drug delivery. Even though he wasn't a drug user, it seemed like fast and easy money. In addition to the usual speakers and educational programs provided in your school and community on these topics, have students do further research on various aspects of drugs such as mandatory sentencing for specific quantities, birth defects related to crack and cocaine, drug-related crime for habit support, and so on.

Consult books such as the following: Gilda Berger's *Straight Talk About Drugs* (Millbrook, 1991), *Know About Drugs* by Margaret O. Hyde (Walker, 1990), *Drugs in America* by Michael Kronenwetter (Messner, 1991), *Drugs and You* by Arnold Madison (Messner, 1990), *Drugs on Your Streets* by Gabrielle Edwards (Rosen, 1991), and *Addicted, in Their Own Words: Kids Talking About Drugs* as told to Joel Engel (Tor Books, 1990).

The following materials can be used for information on the use of drugs in sports: Michael J. Asken's *Dying to Win: The Athlete's Guide to Safe and Unsafe Drugs in Sports* (Acropolis, 1988), Edward F. Dolan's *Drugs in Sports* (Franklin Watts, 1992), *Steroids* by Hank Nuwer (Franklin Watts, 1990), and *Steroids: Big Muscles, Big Problems* by Alvin Silverstein et al. (Enslow, 1992). Also provide the following videos: *Athletes & Addiction: It's Not a Game* (Coronet/MTI Film & Video, 1991) and *Steroids: Shortcut to Make-Believe Muscles* (Film Ideas, 1988).

Sociology/Native Americans—Uncle Jake fears that Sonny will lose touch with Indian culture, but the youth faces a poor economic future on the reservation. The 1990s find local, state, and federal governments still grappling with the issues of Indian sovereignty, treaty rights and violations, and the right to make economic decisions without government intervention. Issues such as reservation gambling, fishing rights, religious freedom, and Indian health problems can be researched to give students a better understanding of the problems facing Native American communities.

Topical books include *To Live in Two Worlds: American Indian Youth Today* by Brent K. Ashabranner and Paul Conklin (Dodd, Mead, 1984), *The Nations Within: The Past and Future of American Indian Sovereignty* by Vine Deloria and Clifford M. Lytle (Pantheon Books, 1984), *Rising Voices: Writings of Young Native Americans* selected by Arlene B. Hirschfelder and Beverly R. Singer (Scribner Books for Young Readers, 1992), and *Tribal Assets: The Rebirth of Native America* by Robert H. Write (Henry Holt, 1990). An excellent reference tool is *Through Indian Eyes: The Native Experience in Books for Children* edited by Beverly Slapin and Doris Seale (New Society, 1992).

Sports/Boxing—Boxing is considered controversial by some people. In the 1990s, the violence of this sport has been examined in light of the Mike Tyson rape controversy. In the 1980s, the physical damage suffered by boxers was brought to the attention of the general public because of the obvious physical deterioration of former world heavyweight boxing champion Mohammed Ali. There are differences between Olympic boxing and professional boxing. Students can research these differences and the rules of the sport by using current periodicals and indexes as well as *Rules of the Game* by the Diagram Group (St. Martin's Press, 1990).

Robert Lipsyte Wrote:

Assignment Sports

The Brave

The Chemo Kid

The Chief

The Contender

Free to Be Mohammed Ali

Jock and Jill

Liberty Two

The Masculine Mystique

Nigger

One Fat Summer

Something Going (with Steve Cady)

Sportsworld: An American Dreamland

Summer Rules

The Summerboy

Native American Teens

Borland, Hal. *When Legends Die*

Cannon, A. E. *The Shadow Brothers*

Highwater, Jamake. *Eyes of Darkness*

——. *I Wear the Morning Star*

Hobbs, Will. *Bearstone*

Lipsyte, Robert. *The Brave*

——. *The Chief*

Paulsen, Gary. *Canyons*

Reaver, Chap. *A Little Bit Dead*

Sports

Cannon, A. E. *The Shadow Brothers*

Crutcher, Chris. *Running Loose*

——. *Stotan!*

Davis, Terry. *Vision Quest*

Dygard, Thomas. *Quarterback Walk-on*

Klass, David. *Wrestling with Honor*

Lipsyte, Robert. *The Brave*

——. *The Chief*

——. *The Contender*

Miklowitz, Gloria D. *Anything to Win*

Shaara, Michael. *For Love of the Game*

Todd, Leonard. *Squaring Off*

Lyons, Mary E.

Sorrow's Kitchen: The Life and Folklore of Zora Neale Hurston

LC 90-8058, ©1990, 125p., $13.95 (ISBN 0-684-19198-9), Scribner Books for Young Readers

Genres: Biography, folktale, multicultural

Themes: Writers, folklore, black culture, love, strife, death, friendship, determination, storytelling, education, anthropology, voodoo, zombies, Harlem Renaissance, racism, integration

Reading level: Seventh grade

Interest level: Seventh through twelfth grades

Reviews:
Booklist. 87(8):816 December 15, 1990
Bulletin of the Center for Children's Books.
    44(5):124 January, 1991. (Recommended)
Horn Book. 67(2): 216 March/April, 1991.
    (Starred)
School Library Journal. 37(1):119 January,
    1991. (Starred)
Voice of Youth Advocates. 13(6):378 February,
    1991. (#4 quality, #2 popularity)

Author Information

A school librarian, Mary E. Lyons lives in Charlottesville, Virginia. She became interested in women writers when she was a reading teacher in a middle school and discovered that women writers were underrepresented in books for her students. Lyons received two grants from the University of Virginia and used them to develop materials on women writers. *Sorrow's Kitchen* is her first book for young adults. She has also written *A Story of Her Own: A Resource Guide to Teaching Literature by Women* (Heartwood Books, 1985), *Raw Head, Bloody Bones: African-American Tales of the Supernatural* (Scribner Books for Young Readers, 1991), *Starting Home: The Story of Horace Pippin, Painter* (Charles Scribner's Sons, 1993), *Stitching Stars: The Story Quilts of Harriet Powers* (Charles Scribner's Sons, 1993), and *Letters from a Slave Girl: The Story of Harriet Jacobs* (Scribner Books for Young Readers, 1992).

Plot Summary

Half biography and half fiction (Hurston's own), this is a chronicle of the life of Zora Neale Hurston, whose writing and research preserved valuable African-American folktales. Hurston struggled to receive an education, make a living, work as an anthropologist, and be accepted as a leading black writer during the Harlem Renaissance. In this biography, each chapter explores a specific period of Hurston's life and is followed by well-chosen selections of her own writing. Photographs of Hurston are sprinkled liberally throughout the text. Also included are notes of quotations, a suggested reading list, a bibliography, and an index.

Introducing the Book

This succinct and lively biography is a good choice for that perennial biography requirement. Hurston's own writing and experiences researching voodoo and zombies will especially appeal to reluctant readers. To hook potential readers, read aloud Hurston's story of zombies and "The Case of Felicia Felix-Mentor" (Pp. 84-89, hardback edition). This title was included on the 1992 ALA/YALSA Recommended Books for the Reluctant Young Adult Reader list.

Booktalks

In the Aisle

Zombies, voodoo, and black folktales highlight this biography of a brave and outrageous woman. Growing up in a time when both women and blacks struggled for equality, Zora Neale Hurston bucked the tide and became a noted writer and researcher whose work today is recognized as fascinating and important.

With the Author's Words

Zora Neale Hurston was a woman who was not afraid to be outrageous. She was wild and unpredictable, and stories about her odd behavior abounded.

> *To disprove the popular notion that blacks' skulls were too small to hold normal-size brains, she stood on a street corner and measured the heads of complete strangers. And she once took a nickel from a blind man's cup, saying, "I need money worse than you today. Lend me this! Next time I'll give it back."* (Pp. 37-39, hardback edition)

Hurston was indeed often short of funds and struggled to make ends meet. Her research and writing about African-American folklore include accounts of zombies and voodoo magic, which actually scared the wits out of her. Do you dare read *Sorrow's Kitchen*?

Literature Extensions/Alternative Book Report Activities

Anthropology—Zora Neale Hurston's work as an anthropologist is recognized as critically important in the preservation and understanding of African-American culture. Interested students can learn more about anthropological research by looking at specific work done in the field. Examples include the recent excavation of the Old Negro Burial Ground discovered in New York City. Anthropologists studying this site are discovering proof of a Colonial-era black community that has not been historically documented. Other students may wish to learn more about the "Iceman," a Stone Age wanderer found in Europe in 1991. He was carbon-dated to be approximately 5,300 years old.

Supplementary materials include the *Encyclopedia of Anthropology* (Harper & Row, 1976) and *The White Lantern* by Evan S. Connell (North Point, 1989), as well as books and articles relating to Margaret Mead and the Leakey family.

English/Composition—In addition to *Sorrow's Kitchen*, several other Hurston biographies have recently been published: *Jump at de Sun: The Story of Zora Neale Hurston* by A. P. Porter (Carolrhoda Books, 1992), *Zora Neale Hurston: A Storyteller's Life* by Janelle Yates (Ward Hill Press, 1992), *Zora Neale Hurston: Writer and Storyteller* by Patricia C. McKissack and Frederick McKissack (Enslow, 1992), *Zora! Zora Neale Hurston: A Woman and Her Community* edited by N. Y. Nathiri (Sentinel Communications, 1991), and *Zora Neale Hurston* by Paul Witcover (Chelsea House, 1990).

Students interested in further reading about Hurston can compare and contrast the treatments in these other sources. Refer to the bibliography in Lyons's book (Pp. 137-39) for further writings about Hurston.

Folklore/Storytelling—As in most cultures, the oral tradition of storytelling is important in African-American cultures. Hurston's preservation of some of these unique tales is a fascinating part of *Sorrow's Kitchen*.

Interested students can explore this further by learning storytelling techniques from books such as *Every Child a Storyteller* by Harriet R. Kinghorn and Mary Helen Pelton (Libraries Unlimited, 1991), Caroline Feller Bauer's *Read for the Fun of It: Active Programming with Books for Children* (H.E. Wilson, 1992), *Storytelling for Young Adults: Techniques and Treasury* by Gail de Vos (Libraries Unlimited, 1991), *Storytelling: Process and Practice* by Norma J. Livo and Sandra A. Rietz (Libraries Unlimited, 1986), and *Twice Upon a Time* by Judy Sierra and Robert Kaminski (H. W. Wilson, 1989). Some students may wish to learn tales and stage a storytelling festival for elementary schools or public libraries.

Provide collections of black folktales suitable for reading or telling. Include Virginia Hamilton's *The All Jahdu Storybook* (Harcourt Brace Jovanovich, 1991) and *The People Could Fly: American Black Folktales* (Alfred A. Knopf, 1985), Patricia C. McKissack's *The Dark-Thirty: Southern Tales of the Supernatural* (Alfred A. Knopf, 1992) and McKissack's collaboration with Ruthilde Kronberg titled *A Piece of the Wind and Other Stories to Tell* (Harper & Row, 1990), *Afro-American Folktales: Stories from Black Traditions in the New World* edited by Roger D. Abrahams (Pantheon Books, 1985), *Storytelling Folklore Sourcebook* by Norma J. Livo and Sandra A. Rietz (Libraries Unlimited, 1991), and Mary E. Lyons's own *Raw Head, Bloody Bones: African-American Tales of the Supernatural* (Scribner, 1992). Students can find and identify familiar folktale motifs such as John and Massa lies, Jack tales, and creation stories.

History/African-Americans—Hurston was a member of the Harlem Renaissance, the first artistic and intellectual movement that brought African-Americans to the attention of the wider public. During the 1920s the most important individuals in the Harlem Renaissance were Langston Hughes, Jean Toomer, Countee Cullen, Claude McKay, Eric Waldron, Arna Bontemps, and Richard Wright. Interested students may wish to read biographical accounts of these black artists and intellectuals.

Explore other examples of contributions to the United States by the African-American community. Provide materials such as *Black Olympian Medalists* by James A. Page (Libraries Unlimited, 1991), Jim Haskins's *Outward Dreams: Black Inventors and Their Inventions* (Bantam Books, 1991), *Against All Opposition: Black Explorers in America* (Walker, 1992), *One More River to Cross: The Stories of Twelve Black Americans* (Scholastic, 1992), *Now Is Your Time! The African-American Struggle for Freedom* by Walter Dean Myers (HarperCollins, 1991), *Growing Up Black: From Slave Days to the Present—25 African-Americans Reveal the Trials and Triumphs of Their Childhoods* edited by Jay David (Avon Books, 1992), and *Chronology of African-American History: Significant Events and People from 1619 to the Present* by Alton Hornsby, Jr. (Gale Research, 1991).

115

Multicultural Authors

Angelou, Maya

Erdrich, Louise

Guy, Rosa

Hamilton, Virginia

Hurston, Zora Neale

Morrison, Toni

Tan, Amy

Uchida, Yoshiko

Walker, Alice

Woodson, Jacqueline

Yep, Lawrence

American Folktales

Cohen, Daniel. *Southern Fried Rat & Other Gruesome Tales*

Hamilton, Virginia. *The All Jahdu Storybook*

————. *The People Could Fly: American Black Folktales*

Jagendorf, M. A. *Folk Stories of the South*

Lester, Julius. The Uncle Remus series

Lyons, Mary E. *Raw Head, Bloody Bones: African-American Tales of the Supernatural*

McKissack, Patricia C. *The Dark-Thirty: Southern Tales of the Supernatural*

Steele, Phillip W. *Ozark Tales and Superstitions*

Black Women of Distinction

Biracree, Tom. *Althea Gibson: Tennis Champion*

————. *Wilma Rudolph*

Blue, Rose, and Corine Naden. *Barbara Jordan*

Dallard, Shyrlee. *Ella Baker: A Leader Behind the Scenes*

Friese, Kai. *Rosa Parks: The Movement Organizes*

Henry, Sondra, and Emily Taitz. *Coretta Scott King: Keeper of the Dream*

Koral, April. *Florence Griffith Joyner: Track and Field Star*

Lyons, Mary E. *Sorrow's Kitchen: The Life and Folklore of Zora Neale Hurston*

McKissack, Patricia C., and Frederick McKissack. *Sojourner Truth: Ain't I a Woman?*

Parks, Rosa (with Jim Haskins). *Rosa Parks: My Own Story*

Rubel, David. *Fannie Lou Hamer: From Sharecropping to Politics*

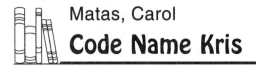

Matas, Carol
Code Name Kris

LC 90-32656, ©1989, 152p., $12.95 (ISBN 0-684-19208-X), Scribner Books for Young Readers. Paperback $2.95 (ISBN 0-590-45034-4), Scholastic

Genre: Historical fiction, multicultural

Themes: Danish resistance, World War II, Jews, Nazis, friendship, courage, danger, guilt, sacrifice, unity, death, underground newspapers, journalism, sabotage, torture, love, hate, patriotism

Reading level: Sixth grade

Interest level: Seventh through twelfth grades

Reviews:
Bulletin of the Center for Children's Books. 44(5):124-25 January, 1991. (Recommended)
Horn Book. 67(1):74-75 January/February, 1991
School Library Journal. 36(12):121-22 December, 1990
Voice of Youth Advocates. 13(6):354 February, 1991. (#4 quality, #4 popularity)

Author Information

Full-time writer Carol Matas lives with her husband and two children in Winnipeg, Ontario, Canada. Holding a degree in English literature from the University of Western Ontario, Matas conducts workshops and visits schools.

Plot Summary

This sequel to *Lisa's War* (Scholastic, 1989) features Jesper, whose code name is Kris. It is an accounting of his actions as a member of the Danish resistance during World War II. Captured by the Nazis, Jesper recounts the events leading up to his imprisonment and torture. His primary contribution to the resistance is as a journalist for the underground press. When his good friend Stefan returns from hiding, Jesper joins him in a major saboteur effort.

Introducing the Book

The teaching of historical events is always enhanced with the use of historical fiction. *Code Name Kris* is a perfect book to tie in with a history unit on World War II. Reading aloud the first chapter will firmly hook students. The action is immediate and intense.

Booktalks

In the Aisle

Jesper has joined the Danish resistance movement to fight against the Nazi occupation. His job is to cover stories for the underground newspaper. His future is uncertain; he's frequently in danger and always on the move. The fate of Danish Jews and the future of his country hang in the balance.

With the Author's Words

This is how *Code Name Kris* begins:

> *I am to be executed. It will be soon. The Nazis are getting desperate, and as they get more desperate they get meaner. I've been alone in this cell for two weeks now.... I'm allowed one last letter, a farewell letter to my family. The guard laughed. He knows I can't write. They pulled all my fingernails out and my fingers are swollen and bleeding. But I can think. They can't stop that.* (P. 1, hardback edition)

This book contains Jesper's thoughts and the memories of his years in the Danish resistance movement as he fought against the Nazi occupation of Denmark.

Literature Extensions/Alternative Book Report Activities

Journalism—As Jesper relates the story of his activities with the underground newspaper, he struggles to do what every good news reporter must do: "sort through the facts, pick and choose what's important, put things in order" (P. 42, hardback edition). If students in your classroom were writing for an underground paper, what would they write about? Their news stories should reflect Jesper's advice.

Psychology/Prison—Throughout Jesper's imprisonment he is able to survive because he realizes the Nazis can't keep him from thinking. Other prisoners have devised numerous methods to maintain their sanity and pass the time. Prisoners frequently developed codes that enabled them to communicate with each other. Traditional codes such as Morse codes have been used, in addition to contrived codes like eye blinking. Students can learn codes, make up their own, or simply read more about them.

Provide *Loads of Codes and Secret Ciphers* by Paul B. Janeczko (Macmillan, 1984), E. A. Grant's *The Book of Secret Codes, Signals and Ciphers* (Running Press, 1989), and *Writing Secret Codes and Sending Secret Messages* by Gyles Brandreth (Sterling, 1986). For further research on prisoners who developed ingenious survival methods, students can consult periodical indexes for references to the American hostages imprisoned in Lebanon and released in 1991.

Social Studies/Newspapers—In order for Danish citizens to stay informed about the war and the Nazi occupation of their country, they relied on underground newspapers. Throughout history this avenue of communication has often been a central factor in defeating the enemy.

Lloyd Alexander's novel *Westmark* (Dutton Children's Books, 1981) is a fictionalized account of the importance an underground press plays in the freedom of a mythical country. Students can read this and explore the larger issue of freedom of the press by consulting books such as *Politics and the Press* by Michael Kronenwetter (Franklin Watts, 1987).

World History—Using *Code Name Kris* as a starting point, expand the study to include a look at other materials on resistance efforts. Consider using Nathaniel Benchley's *Bright Candles: A Novel of the Danish Resistance* (Harper, 1974), *Anne Frank Remembered* by Miep Gies and Allison Gold (Simon & Schuster, 1987), *Resistance Movements* by R. Conrad Stein and Robert L. Messner (Childrens Press, 1988), *That Denmark Might Live: The Saga of the Danish Resistance in World War II* by Irving Werstein (Macrae Smith, 1967), *The Resistance* by Russell Miller (Time Life, 1979), *Upon the Head of the Goat: A Childhood in Hungary, 1939-1944* by Aranka Siegal (Farrar, Straus & Giroux, 1981), *Sinister Touches: The Secret War Against Hitler* by Robert Goldston (Dial Press, 1982), and *Life with the Enemy: Collaboration and Resistance in Hitler's Europe, 1939-1945* by Werner Rings (Doubleday, 1982).

The Holocaust—Nonfiction

Epstein, Helen. *Children of the Holocaust: Conversations with Sons and Daughters of Survivors*

Frank, Anne. *Anne Frank's Tales from the Secret Annex*

Friedman, Ina R. *The Other Victims: First-Person Stories of Non-Jews Persecuted by the Nazis*

Lewin, Rhoda G., ed. *Witness to the Holocaust: An Oral History*

Meltzer, Milton. *Never to Forget: The Jews of the Holocaust*

Miller, Judith. *One, by One, by One: Facing the Holocaust*

Rogasky, Barbara. *Smoke and Ashes: The Story of the Holocaust*

Spiegleman, Art. *Maus*
——. *Maus II*

Toll, Nelly. *Behind the Secret Window: A Memoir of a Hidden Childhood*

Real People, Real Heroes

Atkinson, Linda. *In Kindling Flame*

Friedman, Ina. *Escape or Die: True Stories of Young People Who Survived the Holocaust*

Küchler-Silberman, Lena. *My Hundred Children*

Laska, Vera, ed. *Women in the Resistance and in the Holocaust: The Voices of Eyewitnesses*

Lawson, Don. *The French Resistance*

Meltzer, Milton. *Rescue: The Story of How Gentiles Saved Jews in the Holocaust*

Prager, Arthur, and Emily Prager. *World War II Resistance Stories*

Siegal, Aranka. *Upon the Head of the Goat: A Childhood in Hungary, 1939-1944*

Vinke, Hermann. *The Short Life of Sophie Scholl*

Europe—World War II Fiction

Gallaz, Christopher. *Rose Blanche*

Gehrts, Barbara. *Don't Say a Word*

Laird, Christa. *Shadow of the Wall*

Lingard, Joan. *Tug of War*

Matas, Carol. *Code Name Kris*
——. *Lisa's War*

O'Neil, Denny, and Michael Kaluta. *The Shadow*

Orlev, Uri. *Island on Bird Street*
——. *The Man from the Other Side*

Ramati, Alexander. *And the Violins Stopped Playing: A Story of the Gypsy Holocaust*

Temperley, Alan. *Murdo's War*

Westall, Robert. *Blitzcat*

Murphy, Jim

The Boys' War: Confederate and Union Soldiers Talk About the War

LC 89-23959, ©1990, 110p., $15.95 (ISBN 0-89919-893-7), Clarion Books

Genre: Nonfiction

Themes: U.S Civil War, young soldiers, adventure, diaries, letters, historical photographs, homesickness, battle, discipline, survival, drummers

Reading level: Seventh grade

Interest level: Fifth through twelfth grades

Reviews:
Booklist. 87(7):733 December 1, 1990
Bulletin of the Center for Children's Books. 44(6):126 January, 1991. (Recommended)
Horn Book. 67(1):86-87 January/February, 1991. (Starred)
School Library Journal. 37(1):120 January, 1991. (Starred)
Voice of Youth Advocates. 14(1):60 April, 1991. (#4 quality, #3 popularity)

Author Information

Free-lance editor Jim Murphy has written over a dozen books for young readers. A graduate of Rutgers University and Radcliffe College, Murphy wasn't a big reader as a child, at least not until a high school teacher forbade the reading of *A Farewell to Arms* by Ernest Hemingway. Murphy immediately read it and then continued to read every other so-called "shocking" book he could find. That also started his writing career, which at first consisted primarily of poems. He worked as an editor for Clarion Books and eventually realized his career experiences would lend themselves to books. He loves writing and enjoys researching interesting subjects and giving kids "some unusual bits of information." When he was researching the Civil War period, Murphy decided to write *The Boys' War*. He says, "Their voices brought the Civil War alive in a way no history book ever did." Murphy lives with his wife in New Jersey.

Plot Summary

The Civil War was a grand adventure for thousands of boys sixteen and younger. This book is an accounting of their experiences written through personal narratives and combined with original historical photographs to give an authentic look at the lives of these youngsters. The Civil War was the last war in which large numbers of boys were allowed to fight for the United States. The U.S. government changed enlistment requirements after the Civil War so the lives of children would never again be affected so deeply by a war. The helpful appendixes include an afterword, acknowledgments, sources, a bibliography, and an index.

Introducing the Book

This is an excellent book to use in conjunction with a study of the Civil War in U.S. history classes. The liberal use of authentic photographs, the appealing subject matter (boys fighting in a war), and simple-looking format will convince reluctant readers to give it a try. Reading aloud the first section, called "The War Begins," will whet the appetites of listeners, who will want to know more about the fate of these boys.

Booktalks

In the Aisle

Tens of thousands of boys signed up for an exciting adventure—the American Civil War. Unfortunately, it was the bloodiest war this country has ever been involved in. Read about the boy on this cover and others like him who fought to defend their homes and protect their freedom.

With the Author's Words

It may be hard for you to believe that tens of thousands of boys, age sixteen and younger, fought during the Civil War. Looking for adventure, they often lied about their ages. But sometimes their parents allowed them to enlist.

> *Ned Hutter went to join the Confederate army near his hometown in Mississippi. When the recruitment officer asked his age, Ned told him the truth: " 'I am sixteen next June,' I said.... The officer ordered me out of line and my father, who was behind me, stepped to the table. 'He can work as steady as any man,' my father explained. 'And he can shoot as straight as any who has been signed today. I am the boy's father.' It must have been the way he said the words ... [because] the officer handed me the pen and ordered, 'Sign here. ' "* (P. 11)

Most of these boys were used to hard work on the farm but were unprepared for the brutality and harsh reality of the battlefield. *The Boys' War* is their story.

Literature Extensions/Alternative Book Report Activities

History/Civil War—Assemble a classroom library containing books about various aspects of the Civil War. Encourage students to read several to extend their knowledge beyond textbook presentations.

Notable titles include Russell Freedman's *Lincoln: A Photobiography* (Clarion Books, 1987), *The Long Road to Gettysburg* by Jim Murphy (Clarion Books, 1992), *Voices from the Civil War* by Milton Meltzer (Thomas Y. Crowell, 1989), *Civil War!: America Becomes One Nation* by James I. Robertson, Jr. (Alfred A. Knopf, 1992), *John Ericson and the Inventions of War* by Ann Brophy (Silver Burdett, 1991), *A Separate Battle: Women and the Civil War* by Ina Chang (Lodestar, 1991), *The Battle of Gettysburg* by Neil Johnson (Four Winds, 1989), *A Nation Torn* by Delia Ray (Lodestar, 1990), and *Behind Rebel Lines* by Seymour Reit (Harcourt Brace Jovanovich, 1988). Topical novels include *Red Cap* by G. Clifton Wislar (Dutton Children's Books, 1991), *The Red Badge of Courage* by Stephen Crane (Random House, 1980), and *Charley Skedaddle* by Patricia Beatty (Morrow Junior Books, 1987). See bookmark on page 122 for further titles.

A computer program that simulates three Civil War battles is available. Called *Blue Power, Grey Smoke* (Core Group), this software challenges players to use their knowledge of history and planning ability to select weapons, field supplies, military tactics, and so on.

History/Letters—Letters written to loved ones during wartime accurately reflect the toll a war takes. During the Civil War, long-distance communication was carried out by letters. Students can examine collections of letters to gain a new perspective on their study of the Civil War. Perhaps they can carry on a return correspondence with a historical letter writer.

Books that contain letters written throughout the Civil War include *The Brother's War: Civil War Letters to Their Loved Ones from the Blue and the Gray* edited by Annette Tapert (Times Books, 1988), *All for the Union: The Civil War Diary and Letters of Elisha Hunt Rhodes* edited by Robert Hart Rhodes (Orion Books, 1991), *Letters in American History: Words to Remember* by Jack Lang (Crown, 1982), *Letters from a Slave Girl: The Story of Harriet Jacobs* by Mary E. Lyons (Scribner Books for Young Readers, 1992), *Becca's Story* by James D. Forman (Scribner Books for Young Readers, 1992), and *Women as Letter Writers* by Richard Ingpen (Telegraph Books, 1981). A related book is *Dear America: Letters Home from Vietnam* edited by Bernard Edelman (W. W. Norton, 1985).

Media/Video/Film—Check with your local library for the PBS documentary series *The Civil War*. A companion book is *The Civil War: An Illustrated History* by Geoffrey C. Ward et al. (Alfred A. Knopf, 1990). A video store will most likely have a copy of the film *Glory* (RCA/Columbia Pictures, 1990). This excellent movie tells the story of the first black regiment to fight in the Civil War, the Massachusetts 54th. Another video is *The Massachusetts 54th Colored Infantry* (PBS Video, 1992). An accompanying book is *Undying Glory* by Clinton Cox (Scholastic, 1991).

For a treasury of reading and video viewing, investigate the Rand McNally series *The Civil War Battlefield Guide*, *Gettysburg Battlefield Tour*, *Touring Civil War Battlefields*, and *The Civil War Wall Chart*, as well as *Echoes of the Blue & Gray Videos* produced by Civil War buff William B. Styple.

Sports/Baseball—One letter home from a captive boy soldier talked about a game the prisoners played that they called "base-ball." He wrote: "I don't understand the game, as there is a great deal of running and little apparent gain, but those who play it get very excited over it, and it appears to be fine exercise" (P. 85). How did baseball get started? Was this the historic beginning?

Provide students with the following references: *The Story of Baseball* by Lawrence S. Ritter (Morrow Junior Books, 1990), *The History of National League Baseball Since 1876* by Glenn Dickey (Scarborough House, 1982), *The Story of Baseball* by John Durant (Hastings House, 1973), and *A Hundred and Fiftieth Anniversary Album of Baseball* by Harvey Frommer (Franklin Watts, 1988).

Related videos are *Forever Baseball* (PBS Video) and *The History of Baseball Video* (Major League Baseball Productions).

122

Jim Murphy Wrote:

The Boys' War

Custom Car: A Nuts & Bolts Guide to Building One

Guess Again: More Weird & Wacky Inventions

The Last Dinosaur

The Long Road to Gettysburg

Napoleon Lajoic: Modern Baseball's First Superstar

Tractors: From Yesterday's Steam Wagons to Today's Turbo-charged Giants

Two Hundred Years of Bicycles

True Accounts from the Civil War

Brophy, Ann. *John Ericson and the Inventions of War*

Chang, Ina. *A Separate Battle: Women and the Civil War*

Cox, Clinton. *Undying Glory*

Freedman, Russell. *Lincoln: A Photobiography*

Johnson, Neil. *The Battle of Gettysburg*

Meltzer, Milton. *Voices from the Civil War*

Murphy, Jim. *The Boys' War*

———. *The Long Road to Gettysburg*

Ray, Delia. *A Nation Torn*

Reit, Seymour. *Behind Rebel Lines*

Robertson, James I., Jr. *Civil War! America Becomes One Nation*

Tapert, Annette, ed. *The Brother's War: Civil War Letters to Their Loved Ones from the Blue and the Gray*

Civil War Stories

Beatty, Patricia. *Charley Skedaddle*

———. *Jayhawker*

Clapp, Patricia. *The Tamarack Tree*

Collier, James Lincoln, and Christopher Collier. *My Brother Sam Is Dead*

Crane, Stephen. *The Red Badge of Courage*

Forman, James. *My Enemy, My Brother*

Hunt, Irene. *Across Five Aprils*

Hurmence, Belinda. *A Girl Called Boy*

Lunn, Janet. *The Root Cellar*

Morris, Gilbert. *The Last Confederate*

Rinaldi, Ann. *The Last Silk Dress*

Shore, Laura. *The Sacred Moon Tree*

Shura, Mary Frances. *Gentle Annie: The True Story of a Civil War Nurse*

Sterling, Dorothy. *Captain of the Planter*

Wisler, G. Clifton. *Red Cap*

Nixon, Joan Lowery
Whispers from the Dead

LC 89-15555, ©1989, 180p., $14.95 (ISBN 0-385-29809-9), Delacorte Press. Paperback $3.50 (ISBN 0-440-20809-2), Dell

Genres: Mystery, supernatural, contemporary realistic fiction

Themes: Near-death experiences, psychic abilities, drownings, ghostly communications, secrets, murder, moving, friendship, family relationships, haunted houses

Reading level: Fifth grade

Interest level: Seventh through twelfth grades

Reviews:
Booklist. 86(2):164 September 15, 1989
School Library Journal. 35(13):275-76 September, 1989. (Starred)
Voice of Youth Advocates. 12(5):280 December, 1989. (#3 quality, #4 popularity)

Author Information

Born in Los Angeles in 1927, Joan Lowery Nixon has moved around the West with her husband, Hershell, who is a petroleum geologist. The Nixons have collaborated on many science books. Including these, Joan Lowery Nixon has authored more than sixty titles, two-thirds of which are mysteries. She graduated from the University of Southern California with a journalism degree but found herself teaching kindergarten and enjoyed that so much she went back to school to obtain a teacher's certificate. Nixon has been writing articles since she was seventeen. After attending her first writers' conference in 1961, she was inspired to begin writing for children. *The Mystery of Hurricane Castle* (Criterion, 1964), was written at the urging of two of her children, whom Nixon included as characters. She loves to write books with a hopeful message for children and likes to include some humor in her suspenseful books to break the tension. Nixon lives in Houston, Texas, and continues to teach and write. She is a charter member of the Society of Children's Book Writers and is a member and past officer of the Mystery Writers of America.

Plot Summary

A near-death drowning experience leaves sixteen-year-old Sarah in touch with the spirit world. When her family moves to a new home, Sarah hears whispering. After she discovers that a murder had occurred in the house, the spiritual contacts become more intense and more important. Seemingly by chance, Sarah meets Tony, an intense and exciting boy. Flattered by his attention, Sarah does not realize the danger she is in until it is almost too late.

Introducing the Book

Read aloud the first two paragraphs of the prologue to capture the attention of potential readers. This fast-paced, can't-put-it-down ghost story will keep readers entranced. *Whispers* was included on the 1990 ALA/YALSA Recommended Books for the Reluctant Young Adult Reader list.

Booktalks

In the Aisle

Whispers always attract attention. And when no one is present but you, where do the whispers come from? From the dead? What kind of a person can hear *Whispers from the Dead*? Sarah can, in this Joan Lowery Nixon thriller.

With the Author's Words

When Sarah's family moves to a new town and a new house, her mother is delighted but Sarah isn't.

> *"Oh!" Mom said, staring up at the high ceiling. "This is beautiful!" But I couldn't move. I felt as though I'd been sucked into a cold, smothering mist that surged forward, its thudding heartbeat racing, pounding against my forehead like hammer blows. The echo of a scream beat against my mind, and I gasped in panic.... "Sarah," Mom said, "What is it? You're trembling."... I didn't stop to think. "It's this house," I whispered.* (P. 12, hardback edition)

Since her near-drowning, Sarah has been having psychic experiences. Something awful has happened in this house, and Sarah's about to hear *Whispers from the Dead*.

Literature Extensions/Alternative Book Report Activities

Government/Immigration/Illegal Aliens—The murder victim in this novel was an illegal Mexican immigrant. The issue of immigration is always topical. Students can find out more by referring to *Coming to America: A History of Immigration and Ethnicity in American Life* by Roger Daniels (Harper, 1990), *The Essential Immigrant* by Dan Lacey (Hippocrene Books, 1990), *Illegal Aliens* by Pierre Hauser (Chelsea House, 1990), *The Uncertain Journey: Stories of Illegal Aliens in El Norte* by Margaret Poynter (Atheneum, 1992), and *MexAmerica: Two Countries, One Future* by Lester D. Langley (Crown, 1988). Students can obtain current information by using *Readers' Guide to Periodical Literature* and *Facts on File*.

Health/CPR—Sarah's life is saved when a life guard administers CPR. Do your students know this important life-saving technique? Invite an expert (Red Cross representative, physician, paramedic, or nurse) to your classroom to demonstrate regular CPR and infant CPR.

Collect some written material with illustrations such as Mary Kittredge's *Emergency Medicine* (Chelsea House, 1991), Greg Kuehl's *CPR: The Way to Save Lives* (J. D. Heade, 1984), and materials from the American Red Cross to reinforce demonstrations.

Psychology/Psychic/Near-Death Experiences—After Sarah's near-death experience, she seems to be closely attuned to the spirit world. Interested students may want to do further reading about the interesting phenomenon of near-death experiences.

Provide books such as *The Light Beyond* by Raymond A. Moody and Paul Perry (Bantam Books, 1988), *Life After Life: The Investigation of a Phenomenon, Survival of Bodily Death* by Raymond A. Moody (Phoenix Press, 1987), *Life at Death: A Scientific Investigation of the Near-Death Experience* by Kenneth Ring (Coward-McCann, 1980), *Closer to the Light: Learning from Children's Near-Death Experiences* by Melvin Morse and Paul Perry (Villard Books, 1990), *The Omega Project: Near Death Experiences, UFO Encounters, and Mind at Large* by Kenneth Ring (William Morrow, 1992), and Time Life's *Psychic Voyages* (1987).

Other materials dealing with psychic experiences are *Psychic Animals: A Fascinating Investigation of Paranormal Behavior* by Dennis Bardens (Henry Holt, 1989) and *The Psychic Detectives: The Story of Psychometry and Paranormal Crime Detection* by Colin Wilson (Berkley, 1987)

Research—In order to find out more about the actual murder that took place in her house, Sarah visits her local library and reads the newspaper accounts of the crime. Most libraries have their local newspapers stored on microfilm, microfiche, or hard copy, and many libraries have indexes to these materials. Students can choose an event or time period and research happenings through local newspapers.

Joan Lowery Nixon Wrote:

Caught in the Act

The Dark and Deadly Pool

Days of Fear

The Ghosts of Now

Land of Hope

The Other Side of the Dark

Secret, Silent Screams

Whispers from the Dead

Scary Stuff— Haunted Houses

Curran, Robert, et al. *The Haunted: One Family's Nightmare*

Herbert, James. *Haunted*

Hoke, Helen, and Franklin Hoke, eds. *Horrifying and Hideous Hauntings: An Anthology*

Jackson, Shirley. *The Haunting of Hill House*

Marsden, Simon. *The Haunted Realm: Ghosts, Spirits and Their Uncanny Abodes*

Myers, Arthur. *The Ghostly Register*

Riccio, Dolores, and Joan Bingham. *Haunted Houses*

Roberts, Nancy. *Haunted Houses: Tales from 30 American Homes*

St. George, Judith. *Haunted*

Williams, Ben, and Jean Williams. *The Black Hope Horror: The True Story of a Haunting*

Wright, T. M. *The School*

R.I.P.

Writers of Chilling Tales

Avi

Bennett, Jay

Bunting, Eve

Christie, Agatha

Clark, Mary Higgins

Cooney, Caroline B.

Duncan, Lois

Holland, Isabelle

Michaels, Barbara

Nixon, Joan Lowery

Rendell, Ruth

Quin-Harkin, Janet

Summer Heat

LC 90-92915, ©1990, 183p., $3.50 (ISBN 0-449-14604-9), Fawcett

Genres: Contemporary realistic fiction, romance

Themes: Friendship, coming of age, single-parent families, love, individuality, boy-girl relationships, acceptance, high school, hopes, gender roles, choices, trust, graduation, rural life, grandmothers, sexual responsibility, music, poetry, travel

Reading level: Sixth grade

Interest level: Ninth through twelfth grades

Reviews:
Voice of Youth Advocates. 13(6):355 February, 1991. (#5 quality, #5 popularity)

Author Information

Janet Quin-Harkin was born in England and came to the United States when she married John Quin-Harkin. She has been a drama teacher and a dance teacher but now writes full time. Quin-Harkin turns out a book every two months and has little trouble coming up with new ideas. Fan mail arrives frequently from all over the world, much of it from girls who "have never read a book before and are now motivated to read more," she says. Quin-Harkin has discovered that girls everywhere have the same hopes and dreams.

Plot Summary

Laurie Beth's future seems certain; after high school graduation she'll marry Crowley and settle down to an unexciting but safe and sure future. That is, until Dylan arrives. His risk taking, creativity, and sense of adventure are appealing and exciting to Laurie Beth. Suddenly the world seems full of choices.

Introducing the Book

Part of the Fawcett for Girls "Portraits Collection," this novel is an ideal choice for the romantically inclined. Sensitive and personal subject matter are realistically portrayed. To launch would-be readers, read aloud the first chapter.

Booktalks

In the Aisle

Can a summer romance completely change your life? That's what Laurie Beth wonders when she has to choose between Crowley, her familiar and stable boyfriend, and the romantic, adventurous Dylan.

With the Author's Words

Laurie Beth is preoccupied as she backs out of her driveway. She's thinking about her upcoming graduation, her boyfriend, Crowley, and her predictable and boring future.

> *I stared in the rearview mirror just a second too long before jamming on the brakes. The bike swerved violently to avoid me. It seemed to fly off the road; then there was a horrible crunch of metal. The next thing I knew the bike was lying on its side in the ditch. Its rider, unidentifiable under a black helmet, was lying a few feet away, not moving.* (P. 28, paperback edition)

The rider is Dylan, and his arrival in Laurie Beth's life spells change and excitement. The summer heats up in *Summer Heat*.

Literature Extensions/Alternative Book Report Activities

Creative Writing/Poetry/Songs—Laurie Beth writes poetry secretly and is willing to share her work only when Dylan tells her of his song writing. Interested students can share their own writings (songs, poems, short stories, essays, etc.) either orally or in a literary magazine.

Provide the following materials for poets: *The Poet's Dictionary: A Handbook of Prosody and Poetic Devices* by William Packard (HarperCollins, 1989), *Written in My Soul* by Bill Flanagan (Contemporary Books, 1986), *Poetspeak: In Their Work, About Their Work: A Selection* by Paul B. Janeczko (Collier, 1991), *The Intimate Art of Writing Poetry* by Ottone Riccio (Prentice-Hall, 1980), *The Poet's Pen: Writing Poetry with Middle and High School Students* by Betty Bonham Lies (Libraries Unlimited, 1993), and *The Young Writer's Handbook* by Susan Tchudi and Stephen Tchudi (Macmillan, 1984).

For songwriters: *Everything You Always Wanted to Know About Songwriting But Didn't Know Who to Ask* by Cliffie Stone and Joan Carol Stone (Showdown Enterprises, 1991) and *The Complete Handbook of Songwriting: An Insider's Guide to Making It in the Music Industry* by Mark Liggett and Cathy Liggett (New American Library, 1985). A computer program called *Music Studio* (Activision) allows students to create and print music and lyrics.

Careers/College Choices—Even though her English teacher encouraged her, Laurie Beth had never seriously considered attending college. Many guides exist to assist students in choosing a career or a college or both. Some of these are the annual *Fiske Guide to Colleges* (Times Books), *Guide to Careers Without College* by Kathleen S. Abrams (Franklin Watts, 1988), *The Encyclopedia of Career Choices for the 1990s* (Putnam, 1991), *Looking Beyond the Ivy League: Finding the Right College for You* by Loren Pope (Viking Penguin, 1990), *The College Guide for Parents* by Charles J. Shields (College Entrance Examination Board, 1988), *The Black College Career Guide* (Zulema Enterprises, 1992), *Coping with Choosing a College* by M. W. Buckalew and L. M. Hall (Rosen, 1990), and *Getting Into College: A Guide for Students and Parents* by Frank C. Leana (Hill & Wang, 1990).

For hints on college applications, refer to *Essays That Worked: 50 Essays from Successful Applications to the Nation's Top Colleges* edited by Boykin Curry and Brian Kashbar (Mustang, 1986) and *On Writing the College Application* by Harry Bauld (Barnes & Noble, 1987).

Career information can be found in *Exploring Careers* edited by JoAnn Amore (Jist Works, 1989), *The New York Times Career Planner* by Elizabeth Fowler (Times Books, 1987), *Guide to Alternative Education and Training* by Vivian DuBrovin (Franklin Watts, 1988), and *Choices: A Student Survival Guide for the 1990s* by Bryna J. Fireside (Garrett Park, 1989).

Science/Weather Forecasting—Laurie Beth is able to predict certain weather patterns fairly accurately because she has grown up where frequent, violent thunderstorms and tornadoes occur. Budding meteorologists may wish to look further into weather prediction. A computer program by MECC for the Apple II called *Five-Star Forecast* and the National Geographic Society's program *Weather Machine* allow students the opportunity to become amateur weather forecasters by putting together a variety of weather variables.

Pertinent books include *Weather Forecasting: A Young Meteorologist's Guide* by Dan Ramsey (TAB Books, 1990), David Ludlum's *The Audubon Society Field Guide to North American Weather* (Alfred A. Knopf, 1991), *The American Weather Book* (American Meteorological Society, 1990), *Weather Forecaster* by Barbara Taylor-Cork (Franklin Watts, 1992), and *Weather and Forecasting* by Storm Dunlop and Francis Wilson (Macmillan, 1982).

Consider inviting a local meteorologist to speak about the career of weather forecasting. Encourage the display and demonstration of weather-predicting tools.

Speech Writing/Public Speaking—Laurie Beth's graduation speech was not selected as the winning speech, but writing it was important to her. Whether or not your school has a similar competition, encourage students to learn speech-writing and delivery techniques.

Provide resources such as *You Mean I Have to Stand Up and Say Something?* by Joan Detz (Macmillan, 1986), *Making Your Point: How to Speak and Write Persuasively* by Robert E. Dunbar (Franklin Watts, 1990), *So You Have to Give a Speech!* by Margaret Ryan (Franklin Watts, 1987), *How to Make a Speech* by Steve Allen (McGraw-Hill, 1986), and *Speak Up! A Guide to Public Speaking* by Patricia Sternberg (Messner, 1987).

128

Expressive Teens: Writers and Musicians

Allen, R. E. *Ozzy on the Outside*

Block, Francesca. *Weetzie Bat*

Brooks, Bruce. *Midnight Hour Encores*

Frank, Elizabeth Bales. *Cooder Cutlas*

Powell, Randy. *Is Kissing a Girl Who Smokes Like Licking an Ashtray?*

Quin-Harkin, Janet. *Summer Heat*

Strasser, Todd. *Rock 'n' Roll Nights*

——. *Turn It Up*

Tamar, Erika. *Blues for Silk Garcia*

Wolff, Virginia Euwer. *The Mozart Season*

Is College for Me?

Cooney, Caroline B. *The Party's Over*

Ferris, Jean. *Across the Grain*

Greenwald, Sheila. *Blissful Joy and the SATs: A Multiple Choice Romance*

Guy, Rosa. *The Music of Summer*

Harrell, Janice. *So Long, Senior Year*

Naylor, Phyllis Reynolds. *The Year of the Gopher*

Quin-Harkin, Janet. *Summer Heat*

Thompson, Julian. *Simon Pure*

Voigt, Cynthia. *Tell Me If Lovers Are Losers*

Williams-Garcia, Rita. *Fast Talk on a Slow Track*

Romance

Cannon, Bettie. *Begin the World Again*

Caseley, Judith. *Kisses*

Clements, Bruce. *Tom Loves Anna Loves Tom*

Guy, Rosa. *The Music of Summer*

Hall, Barbara. *Skeeball and the Secret of the Universe*

Hamilton, Virginia. *A White Romance*

Jaspersohn, William. *Grounded*

Kerr, M. E. *Little, Little*

Klein, Norma. *Just Friends*

Koertge, Ron. *The Boy in the Moon*

Mazer, Harry. *I Love You, Stupid*

Miklowitz, Gloria D. *The Day the Senior Class Got Married*

Quin-Harkin, Janet. *Summer Heat*

Thesman, Jean. *The Rain Catchers*

Wersba, Barbara. *The Farewell Kid*

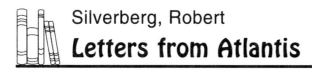

Silverberg, Robert
Letters from Atlantis

LC 90-562, ©1990, 136p., $14.95 (ISBN 0-689-31570-8), Atheneum

Genres: Science fiction, fantasy

Themes: Time travel, dreams, Atlantis, inventions, letter writing, love, friendship, royalty, archaeology, governments, research, extraterrestrials, space travel, racism, disasters

Reading level: Seventh grade

Interest level: Seventh through twelfth grades

Reviews:
Booklist. 87(6):660 November 15, 1990. (Starred)
School Library Journal. 37(3):218 March, 1991
Voice of Youth Advocates. 13(6):367 February, 1991. (#5 quality, #5 popularity)

Author Information
Diverse and prolific author Robert Silverberg has been writing and publishing science fiction since 1955. Silverberg writes extensively in many areas, including archaeology, conservation, history, and the natural sciences in addition to science fiction and fantasy. One of the best known of contemporary science fiction writers, Silverberg has received countless awards and has contributed to shaping the science fiction field into what it is today. His aim: "To communicate a very vivid, strange experience."

Plot Summary
A historical researcher from the twenty-first century, Roy travels back in time into the mind of the eighteen-year-old crown prince of the legendary island, Atlantis. The purpose of this time travel is to discover more about this mysterious island and its civilization. Roy discovers nineteenth-century technology in 18,000 B.C. and wonders how such an advanced civilization can exist in a barbaric world. All this is revealed in letters Roy writes to a fellow time-mind traveler. This book is part of Atheneum's Dragonflight fantasy series written by a variety of notable science fiction-fantasy authors. (See bookmarks on page 131 for other titles.)

Introducing the Book
Read aloud the first chapter to launch this accessible book written on a fascinating topic. The large print, generous margins, and attractive cover will appeal to nearly every reader.

Booktalks

In the Aisle
When you read this book, it's like reading somebody else's mail. The letters are to Lora and they are from Roy, who is currently living inside the mind of the crown prince of Atlantis. As you eavesdrop on their correspondence, you'll find out what really happened to that mysterious island thousands of years ago.

With the Author's Words
Roy is a traveler through time, and he is presently residing inside the mind of the crown prince of Atlantis. For a long while his presence has been a secret, but all that is about to change.

> *Big trouble. The Prince knows I'm here.... [A]t last he spoke—mentally, loud and clear—directly to me. It was like a bomb going off right in my face:—Who are you, demon, and why are you within me?... I was totally stunned. I didn't know what to say or do or think. This was my chance, if ever there was one, to make direct contact with the Prince.* (Pp. 75-76, hardback edition)

Roy's mission is supposed to be secret. He is not, under any circumstances, to make his presence known. But he's been tempted before and is tempted again.

Literature Extensions/Alternative Book Report Activities

English/Writing—This entire novel is presented as a collection of letters. With the prevalence of electronic communications, the art of letter writing seems threatened. Encourage students to continue or begin a correspondence.

The unusual book, *Griffin & Sabine: An Extraordinary Correspondence* by Nick Bantock (Chronicle Books, 1991), *How to Write Irresistible Query Letters* by Lisa Collier Cool (Writer's Digest Books, 1990), and *Lifetime Encyclopedia of Letters* by Harold E. Meyer (Prentice-Hall, 1992) provide examples of excellent letters.

Literature/Greek Mythology—As Silverberg mentions through his protagonist, Roy, the Greek philosopher Plato told of an advanced civilization that flourished on an island in the western sea before it was destroyed by an earthquake (*Timaeus* and *Critias*).

Provide books such as the following for further reading on this fascinating subject: *Atlantis: Opposing Viewpoints* by Wendy Stein (Greenhaven Press, 1989), *Atlantis: The Biography of a Legend* by Marjorie Braymer (Macmillan, 1983), *The Fact or Fiction Files: Lost Civilizations* by Dorothy Hoobler and Thomas Hoobler (Walker, 1992), *Operation Time Search* by Andre Norton (Ballantine Books, 1985), and *Skyborn* by Marcia H. Kruchten (Scholastic, 1989).

Science/Inventions—As Roy becomes more familiar with Atlantis and its citizens, he is amazed at the advanced technology he finds there. The rest of the world is just emerging from the Ice Age, while the people on Atlantis have electricity, steamships, and indoor plumbing. Encourage students to find out more about innovative ideas and inventions. Invite an inventor to class to discuss ideas and patents. Find out about contests in which students can submit their own inventions.

Books on this subject include *The Smithsonian Book of Inventions* (W. W. Norton, 1978), *Inventors and Discoveries: Changing Our World* (National Geographic Society, 1988), *Mousetraps and Muffling Cups: 100 Brilliant and Bizarre United States Patents* by Kenneth Lasson (Arbor House, 1986), *The Inventive Yankee: From Rockets to Roller Skates, 200 Years of Yankee Inventors and Inventions* (Yankee Books, 1989), *I'll Buy That!* by the editors of *Consumer Reports* (Consumer Reports Books, 1986).

Science Fiction/Media Festival—Using books, films, videos, and so on, provide your students with a variety of material focusing on time travel as a theme. The television program "Quantum Leap" has popularized the notion of time travel as a scientific possibility. John W. Macvey's *Time Travel* (Scarborough House, 1990) takes a serious look at time travel and its ramifications. Other materials include H. G. Wells's *The Time Machine*, both the book (Bantam Books, 1984) and the film (MGM/Galaxy, 1960), as well as Mark Twain's *A Connecticut Yankee in King Arthur's Court* (Books of Wonder/Morrow, 1988).

Computer programs *Time Navigator* and *Time Navigator Leaps Back* (MECC) challenge players to travel through American history. Students must navigate by choosing the right clues which include artifacts, headlines, works of literature, and so on.

Stories of Early People

Auel, Jean. Earth's Children series
Bell, Clare. Clan Ground
———. Ratha and Thistle-Chaser
———. Ratha's Creature
Brennan, J. H. Shiva Accused
———. Shiva: An Adventure of the Ice Age
Gear, W. Michael, and Kathleen O'Neal Gear. People of the Earth
———. People of the Fire
———. People of the River
———. People of the Wolf
Harrison, Sue. Mother Earth, Father Sky
Holland, Cecelia. Pillar of the Sky
Kurten, Bjorn. Dance of the Tiger
———. Singletusk
Thomas, Elizabeth Marshall. Reindeer Moon

Time Travel: The Future and the Past Meet

Bellamy, Edward. Looking Backward: 2000-1887
Bond, Nancy. Another Shore
Heinlein, Robert. Time for the Stars
Jones, Diana Wynne. Aunt Maria
Jordan, Sherryl. The Juniper Game
L'Engle, Madeleine. Many Waters
Lisson, Deborah. The Devil's Own
Macevy, John W. Time Travel
MacLeod, Charlotte. The Curse of the Giant Hogweed
Marzollo, Jean. Halfway Down Paddy Lane
Service, Pamela F. The Reluctant God
Simak, Clifford D. The Goblin Reservation
Sleator, William. The Green Futures of Tycho
———. Singularity

The Dragonflight Series—

Novels by noted science fiction and fantasy authors. Each book deals with a major fantasy theme.

Cooper, Louise. The Sleep of Stone
De Lint, Charles. The Dreaming Place
Lee, Tanith. The Black Unicorn
Silverberg, Robert. Letters from Atlantis
Strickland, Brad. Dragon's Plunder
Williams, Tad, and Nina Kiriki Hoffman. Child of an Ancient City

Appendix: Interest and Readability Levels

This listing of the forty titles is arranged by interest levels in hierarchical order. The readability level of each book is to the right of the title entry.

Grades 3-7
Fleischman, Sid. *The Midnight Horse* (4)

Grades 4-7
Yolen, Jane. *Wizard's Hall* (5)

Grades 4-10
Rappaport, Doreen. *Living Dangerously: American Women Who Risked Their Lives for Adventure* (6)

Grades 5-7
Shreve, Susan. *The Gift of the Girl Who Couldn't Hear* (4)

Grades 5-8
Bunting, Eve. *Sharing Susan* (4)
Byars, Betsy. *Bingo Brown, Gypsy Lover* (4)
Cleary, Beverly. *Strider* (4)
Hoover, H. M. *Away Is a Strange Place to Be* (5)
Koller, Jackie French. *If I Had One Wish...* (4)
Spinelli, Jerry. *There's a Girl in My Hammerlock* (4)
Vail, Rachel. *Wonder* (4)

Grades 5-9
Conrad, Pam. *Stonewords: A Ghost Story* (5)
DeFelice, Cynthia. *Weasel* (4)
Fritz, Jean. *Bully for You, Teddy Roosevelt!* (6)
O'Dell, Scott, and Elizabeth Hall. *Thunder Rolling in the Mountains* (5)

Grades 5-10
Service, Pamela. F. *Being of Two Minds* (5)
Woodson, Jacqueline. *The Dear One* (5)

Grades 5-12
Cohen, Daniel. *Ghostly Tales of Love & Revenge* (6)
Murphy, Jim. *The Boys' War* (7)
Tolkien, J. R. R. *The Hobbit* (graphic adaptation) (6)

Grades 6-9
Soto, Gary. *Taking Sides* (5)

Grades 6-12
Paulsen, Gary. *Woodsong* (5)

Grades 7-12
Bennett, Jay. *Coverup* (5)
Bradbury, Ray. *The Ray Bradbury Chronicles 1* (6)
Fleischman, Paul. *The Borning Room* (5)
Grant, Cynthia D. *Keep Laughing* (5)
Hobbs, Will. *Downriver* (6)
Hughes, Monica. *Invitation to the Game* (6)
Klause, Annette Curtis. *The Silver Kiss* (6)
Kuklin, Susan. *What Do I Do Now? Talking About Teenage Pregnancy* (6)
Lipsyte, Robert. *The Brave* (5)
Lyons, Mary. E. *Sorrow's Kitchen: The Life and Folklore of Zora Neale Hurston* (7)
Matas, Carol. *Code Name Kris* (6)
Nixon, Joan Lowery. *Whispers from the Dead* (5)
Silverberg, Robert. *Letters from Atlantis* (7)

Grades 8-12
Block, Francesca Lia. *Witch Baby* (5)
Crutcher, Chris. *Athletic Shorts* (6)

Grades 9-12
Davis, Jenny. *Sex Education* (5)
Koertge, Ron. *The Boy in the Moon* (7)
Quin-Harkin, Janet. *Summer Heat* (6)

Genre Index

Curricular Activities Index

Theme Index

Author Index

Title Index